MANAGEMENT PLANNING FOR THE TWENTY-FIRST CENTURY

MANAGEMENT PLANNING FOR THE TWENTY-FIRST CENTURY

Volume III

(Career Planning and Administration in Government Service)

GIRIRAJ SHAH

GYAN PUBLISHING HOUSE
NEW DELHI-110002

MANAGEMENT PLANNING FOR THE TWENTY-FIRST CENTURY
[*Administration, Behavioural Science, Law, Management*]

ISBN: 81-212-0530-1 (Set)
ISBN: 81-212-0578-6 (Volume III)

Published in 1999 in India by
Gyan Publishing House
5, Ansari Road
New Delhi - 110002

Laser Typeset at Alphabet, Delhi
Printed at Mehra Offset Press, New Delhi.

CONTENTS

PREFACE

The values in the Services have tumbled like a house built of a pack of cards. In fact the worldwide growing disorder and lawlessness are attributed to the falling moral values and standard of policemen's professionalism and the breakdown of the law and order machinery. The helplessness of the administration in the face of mounting political pressure and frequent judicial activism has added the last nail in the coffin. However, the people in power satisfy themselves with occasional rhetoric, preaching high ethics and morals, in the hope that a sermon would work magic and rid the administration of their sins and be a penanced for all troubles without realising that "The administrative machinery is morally depressed, financially starved and badly misused for too long by the politicians and unfortunately, administration has been denied its rightful place both within and outside the government, due to intrigues of the politicians and corrupt administrators with the forces which form part of hand in glove machinations of the government. The ill effects and natural consequences are coming in light in the form of numerous scandals, surfacing not only in India but all over the world. The nexus of the politicians, Administrators and criminals has been exposed only through judicial activism and alertness of some patriotic people. The benign principles of good administration have been thus enumerated in the Gita:

स्वधर्ममपि चावेक्ष्य न विकम्पितुमर्हसि।
धर्म्याद्धि युद्धाच्छ्रेयोऽन्यत्क्षत्रियस्य न विधते।

(Bhagwatgita — Ch. 11-31)

'That is looking at their own Dharmas laid down under the rules, they ought not to waver from it, for there is nothing higher for a Kshatriya than a righteous cause, however, today the average administration not only experiences a void in the existance but also finds his work less rewarding. He realises that he is the target of constant public criticism, his conduct both in public and private is disapproved of at every step and he is accused day in and day out of inefficiency, corruption and insensitivity to the people's welfare. From time to time attention of legislators, politicians, administrators and people posted at places where decision matters, has been drawn from time to time, but not of too much avail.

In this volume I have analysed the administration of Union and state governments, Rule of Law, Conduct and Misconduct, Red-tapism, Bureaucracy, Human Values in Administration, Role of the Human Values and Conduct Rules.

Today everybody seems to be worried about the deteriorating moral standards (Rule of Conduct) in the Service, but not concrete steps have been taken to remove the prevailing ills and nobody has shown a path to lead kindiy light. In the light of my past experiences I have analysed some points in this book which will be helpful for managers and administrators.

No book can be written without drawing source material from books written earlier and listening to personal experiences and even experiences gained during the service. I have also heavily relied on the writing and experiences of my predecessors and colleagues and drawn material from distinguished writers on the subject-like B.N. Lehri, B.N. Mullick, Del Cargne, Prof. Bayley, N.S. Saksena. I have also drawn lessons from Stalwarts like Shanti Prasad, H.K. Kerr, B.S. Bedi and Prakash Singh.

I am thankful to Mr. B.P. Garg for undertaking the stupendous task of publishing this multi-volume project which is probably unique and the first of its kind.

25 March, 1999 **Dr. Giriraj Shah**

ONE

AIDE MEMOIRE ON OFFICIAL BEHAVIOUR

The conduct of government servants in their relation with the public or in the discharge of their duties has in recent years become a subject of frequent discussion. Instances of what is considered improper behaviour on the part of government servants have come to the notice of the government from time to time either in the form of direct complaints from the members of public or through reports from senior officers or as reported in the press. Often, the matter is also discussed in the legislature.

The government is aware that this criticism levelled against its employees is often exaggerated. Sometimes it is entirely baseless. It cannot be denied that government servants have, on occasions, behaved in a manner which is unbecoming of them and which could give rise to valid resentment. It is to be realised also that the function and role of a government servant have undergone considerable change since the attainment of independence. The public servant no longer serves a superimposed foreign government, but a government of the people and thus, the people themselves. The public, therefore, have high expectations from the official machinery and disappointment in this direction is frequently the cause of complaint or criticism.

The government has been viewing the whole question with a somewhat uneasy feeling. While there is no intention to give credence to irresponsible criticism, it is at the same time apparent that widespread criticism of the conduct of public servants is likely to undermine their usefulness and shake the confidence of the public in the governmental machinery. It is essential, therefore, that there should be some broad principles to regulate the behaviour of government servants towards the public and their conduct in the discharge of their duties.

Dealings with the Public

The public are becoming increasingly conscious of their rights. It is essential for any administration to ensure that the public have full confidence in the government servants. Apart from incorruptibility, efficiency and correct behaviour are the two essential requirements of a government servant. Since, the interests of general people are to a great extent affected by the actions of civil servants, it is necessary, for the civil servants to bear in mind that the citizen has a right to expect not only that his matters are dealt with effectively and expeditiously, but also that his personal feelings, no less than his rights, are sympathetically and fairly considered. Delays in the disposal of public matters are a general ground for the complaints and a positive approach has to be made at all levels to ascertain the causes for these delays and also to remove them.

Another important consideration in dealing with common people is a show of courtesy, exercise of patience and a desire to see the other person's point of view. A common man, however humble may be his status in society, expects to be dealt with courteously and to be heard patiently. An attitude of superiority does not help. It merely creates a sense of bitterness which is not good for the administration. It should be remembered that courtesy always pays even if it is not dictated by detailed rules of official etiquette.

Incorruptibility

There have been widespread allegations of corruption against government servants. While it is realised that many of these are exaggerated and some are no more than mere generalisations, it is necessary that an effective drive should be launched by every Head of Department and every Head of Office to ensure that public servants adopt clean methods and are scrupulous in the discharge of their duties. It is possible that at the level at which general people largely come in contact with the official machinery, there is a show of authority, lack of understanding and even corruption in the ranks of government servants. There is need for introspection on this subject on the part of everyone and administrative officers have to satisfy themselves that they are making positive efforts for removing complaints about corruption, whatever the actual position about its extent may be.

Avoidance of Personal Publicity, etc.

It has been noticed that magazines, booklets, etc. published by various departments often contain a profusion of photographs of government officers. Criticism has been made against this practice and there is substance in this criticism. Public funds are not to be utilised for the publicity of officers. These magazines and booklets will serve their purpose better if they describe the activities of the government. Even in cases where departmental work is to be narrated, it would be preferable to lay greater emphasis on the achievements of the departments rather than on the departmental officers. Administrative officers should ensure that the position in this respect is clearly understood by all concerned.

Similar considerations should broadly regulate the conduct of officers in laying foundation stones or in inaugurating functions. It is to be realised in this connection that it will add to the success and effectiveness of government servants themselves if they endeavour to function in anonymity. It is of course not intended that they should not be present at such functions. Actually, participation in them, wherever possible and convenient, would be helpful as their presence is likely to add to the enthusiasm of the people and help them overcome their difficulties. Government servants should not, however, accept the leading role in such functions.

Interdepartmental Harmony

There is much greater need for interdepartmental cooperation and goodwill today than ever before. The functions and responsibilities of government are now much more broad-based. It is impossible for the government machinery to function in watertight compartments. There is need for complete coordination and collaboration amongst various agencies of the government. Interdepartmental rivalries and estrangements become a source of embarrassment to government and hinder the orderly conduct of public business. They also invite ridicule from the public. Differences of opinion can be settled privately with the help of senior officers. But there should be no airing of them in public and government business should not be allowed to suffer on that account.

Detachment from Political Parties

For the proper discharge of their duties, government servants must take a lively interest in the social and economic affairs of the country and it is not intended that they should live in a vacuum. At the same time, government servants have to so conduct themselves in their work and conversation as to leave no room for an impression that they have any alignment with any political party. A government servant, whose duty is to deal with common people, has to make himself accessible to all and deal with them with patience and courtesy and in doing so he has to create an impression of impartiality, fair play and justice. In short, government servants are expected to take an objective view of things, a view which is unconnected with the ideologies of any particular political party. The importance of this rule has to be impressed upon government servants at all levels.

Discipline and Restraint in Discussions and Conversations

There still appears to exist a tendency on the part of government servants for loose and irresponsible talk concerning the affairs and activities of the government. In such talks, personal remarks are sometimes made against political parties, the government and administrative officers. Such talk is derogatory to the prestige, position and reputation of the official who indulges in it, apart from the fact that it is an act of indiscipline and is directly opposed to the government servants' Conduct Rules. A person who does not show respect for those in authority can never expect to command the respect of his own subordinates. Government servants at all levels are expected to behave with a full sense of responsibility in matters of discussion and conversation and this responsibility can be discharged only by exercising the utmost restraint and care.

Senior officers themselves can make their contribution towards the checking of the falling standards of discipline in all spheres of life by adhering to the rules of discipline and thus setting an example. The word 'discipline' is being used here in its wider sense of orderliness, methodical way of doing things, consideration for others and so on. In this sense, unpunctuality, slovenly behaviour and the like would amount to acts of indiscipline. Government servants are expected to be a disciplined body and they are also expected to exhibit better standards of conduct and behaviour than others.

Recreation

Government realises that civil servants, like other hardworking people, should take part in some recreational activities. Recreation is a good and necessary thing and adds to the efficiency and well-being. While everyone is free to select his own form of recreation, there is one general consideration which has to be kept in mind. It is to be ensured that no government servant places himself under any obligation to another person in this matter. There are persons who, from motives of self-interest, are ready to oblige officials and such persons are likely to turn up some day with an unfair or unreasonable request. The rule to be observed in the matter of recreation, therefore, is that all recreation must only be at one's own expense or among friends on a reciprocal basis.

Reception of Criticism

Some officers are inclined to take criticism to heart with the resulting feeling of despondency, while others are entirely impervious to complaints and criticism. Neither of these approaches is correct. Criticism has its value if it is looked at from a proper perspective, that is to say, if it is given an objective approach by subordinating personal feelings even though the criticism may have been expressed in personal terms. If the official, who has been criticised, finds that there is room for improvement on his part, he should welcome the criticism as a reminder to him to change his methods. On the other hand, if he finds that the criticism is without any basis he need not give a second thought to it and at the same time should avoid entertaining feelings of animosity against the persons who made the criticism. If, however, the matters commented upon are such as to require public denial or clarification, the government servant should take prompt steps to do so or, if necessary, refer the matter to government for orders. It is in this way that criticism can be turned to the advantage of the public services.

The Opinion within the Services

We are now apt to forget the value of tradition within the services. Healthy traditions must be established by our senior officers so that there is a sort of public opinion within our own ranks which will discountenance all lapses on the part of individual officer. Fear of losing face among colleagues is perhaps a more effective deterrent than the fear of departmental punishment and it is the duty of all right-thinking government servants to help create the correct opinion within the services.

Conduct yourself Carefully

It is evidently not possible to draw up a catalogue of manners in which a public servant should act in the discharge of his duties. The purpose is, as already stated, to indicate some of the more important principles that should be followed. In matters not covered by the above points the officers will have to decide for themselves how best to act or to conduct themselves in the situations that arise in day-to-day administration. In doing so, it would be well to remember that it is their privilege to serve the interests of the people and that privilege always carries with it great responsibilities. An officer would also do well to remember that his conduct is to be so ordered that it assures, in terms of the preamble to the Constitution, "the dignity of the individual and the unity of the nation."

It is appreciated that these instructions are likely to encroach, to some extent, on the private conduct of government servants also. While there is no intention that government should interfere unduly in the private lives of their employees, it has to be realised that in a welfare state, government activities embrace almost every sphere of human life resulting in a continuous association of government servants with the public. Therefore, it becomes extremely difficult, to demarcate public conduct clearly, from private behaviour. But by acting in the manner suggested, the government servant will earn the gratitude, admiration and respect from the general public.

It was also requested that all possible avenues may be utilised to impress these matters upon those working under the officers or under their guidance. It is necessary to ensure that lapses are taken notice of. If one lapse is ignored, it sets in a chain reaction and disturbs the balance of orderliness. Services do need toning-up. It is essential also to create a proper understanding about the services in the public mind. With tact and sympathetic handling of the staff and ensuring proper standards the present-day administrative difficulties can be overcome and the criticism would die a natural death.

TWO

UNION GOVERNMENT—AN OUTLINE OF ITS ORGANIZATION

The organization of the Union Government as well as of the State Governments is broadly provided for in the Constitution. The Indian Constitution is the federal type, distinguished from the unitary type. In the latter form, the governance of the country is in the hands of a single central authority, for example, the Government of Britain. In the federal type the government is shared matters of countrywide interest being entrusted to a central authority whereas other matters are entrusted to the States. The U.S.A. presents an example of this type of government.

The Indian Constitution provides for the allocation of power to the Centre and States. These powers include legislative, financial (including taxation) and administrative matters. This allocation is made through the three lists contained in the Seventh Schedule of the Constitution:

Union List— This contains subjects within the exclusive purview of the Union—that is, the Parliament and the Union Government.

The State List— Comprises subjects within the exclusive purview of the State Legislatures and the State Governments.

The Concurrent List— This list enumerates the subjects which can be legislated upon by both Parliament and by State Legislatures. But Parliament's law prevails over the State law. A new State law in the Concurrent List, will be operative only if it receives the President's assent.

The subjects reserved exclusively for the Centre include defence, foreign affairs, transport (excluding surface transport) and communications, currency, banking and customs. In the State list are subjects like law and order, education, agriculture, public health, state public works, and irrigation. Amongst the concurrent subjects, mention may be made of industries, labour welfare, price control, electricity and social security, etc.

Emergency Powers

In cases of grave emergency the Union Government has power to invest itself with extraordinary powers of control over State administration subject to the provisions of the Constitution. Such an emergency arises :

(a) when the security of India or a part thereof is threatened, whether by war or by internal disturbance;
(b) where there is a failure of constitutional machinery in the State, that is to say when the Government cannot be carried on by the Council of Ministers;
(c) when the financial stability or credit of India or any part of it is threatened.

When such a situation occurs, the President can issue a proclamation and make necessary consequential provision to deal with the situation in accordance with the provisions of the Constitution. In addition to All-India subjects, the Union Government is also in direct charge of the administration of certain territories known as Union Territories. These are administered by the Centıal Government in the same manner as States are managed by State Governments with a modification that the Legislative powers vest in Parliament.

There are 25 States and 7 Union Territories. The latter include Delhi, Chandigarh, Pondicherry, Daman and Diu, Andaman and Nicobar Islands, Lakshadweep, Dadra and Nagar Haveli.

Administrative Functions

The following authorities come into the picture in the administrative functioning of the Union Government:

(a) President
(b) Prime Minister
(c) Council of ministers and ministries
(d) Central Secretariat and departments
(e) Attached offices
(f) Heads of departments with field offices under them. Each of these is dealt with in a separate section.

The President

The President is the Head of the Indian Union and all exclusive powers are vested in him. Effect to this Constitutional provision, is given by providing, among other things, that all executive actions of the Union will be expressed to have been taken in his name. The President is also the Supreme Commander of the Armed Forces.

A person becomes President through election by an electoral college consisting of the elected members of both Houses of the Union Parliament and the elected members of State Legislative Assemblies. Only a citizen of India of 35 years of age or above is qualified to seek election. He holds office for 5 years and is eligible for re-election.

The President, being the Constitutional Head, acts upon the advice of his Ministers. He is bound by the advice tendered by the Council of Ministers.

The Vice-President

There is a Vice-President though he has no administrative functions except that he acts as a President during a casual vacancy in the office of President. The assigned function of the Vice-President is to act as the ex-officio Chairman of the Rajya Sabha (the Upper House).

The Vice-President is elected by members of electoral college consisting of the members of both Houses of Parliament in accordance with the system of proportional representation by means of the single transferable vote and the voting at such election is by secret ballot. He holds office for 5 years. In order to be eligible for election as Vice-President, a person should among other things, have completed the age of 35 years, which is the same as for the President.

The Prime Minister

In the Constitution of India, as well as in that of the United Kingdom, the Prime Minister occupies a key position. As of Britain, the Indian Prime Minister is normally the leader of the majority party in the Lower House—the House of the People and wields all the authority which appertains to that position. It is only in a nominal manner that the President exercises the executive powers of the Union in day-to-day affairs; the *de facto* head of the central executive is the Prime Minister. It is upon his advice that the wide powers vested in the Central Government are exercised and these powers include the powers of the President in national emergency also.

The Prime Minister's Position

"The Prime Minister", said John Morley, "is the key-stone of the Cabinet Arch." But Sir Ivor Jennings said, "It would, however, be more accurate to describe the Prime Minister as the key-stone of the Constitution." Explaining the position of the Prime Minister vis-a-vis the Cabinet, Lord Morley stated: "Although in Cabinet all its members stand on an equal footing, speak with equal voice and on rare occasions when a decision is taken, are counted on the fraternal principle of one man one vote, yet the head of the Cabinet is the Prime Minister and occupies a position which, so long as it lasts, is one of exceptional and peculiar authority." Lord Morley went on to add, "The flexibility of the Cabinet system allows the Prime Minister to take upon himself a power not inferior to that of a dictator, provided always that the House of Commons will stay by him."

The Prime Minister's power, according to Sir Ivor Jennings, depends in part on his personality, in part on his personal prestige and in part upon his party's support... He appoints and dismisses ministers..., he exercises a wide patronage... He is constantly consulted by ministers on the major problems of their departments..."

The office of the Prime Minister is what its holder chooses to make of it, said Lord Oxford. Personality undoubtedly plays a great part in determining the power of a Prime Minister. The Prime Minister's position as a political leader has been explained by Sir Ivor Jennings in these words, "... the Prime Minister has to give leadership, particularly during a general election when much depends on his personality, prestige and even energy, for though electioneering effects few conversions, it forces the waverers to decide whether to vote or not. There is, however, always an election round the corner and the Prime Minister has to pay special attention to the popularity of his government and the moods of public opinion. If it seems to be losing support, he has to consider whether to reverse the policy, to change its emphasis by starting a new and more popular line, or to send out his golden-voiced orators to prove to the electorate that it has been mistaken."

Council of Ministers

"The growth of special interest, each claiming for itself a representative minister in the Cabinet, has turned it into a noun of multitude and a noun not wholly favourable to the concentrated deliberation which was possible when Pitt had first six, then seven colleagues, Peel twelve and Gladstone fourteen. Today we are a score."[1]

The Council of Ministers is constituted by the President to aid and advise him in the exercise of his functions. It is headed by the Prime Minister who is appointed by the President with Ministers appointed on the advice of the Prime Minister. The Council is collectively responsible to the House of the People which means that it continues in office for so long as it enjoys the confidence of that body.

No court of law can enquire whether any, and if so, what advice was tendered to the President. Irrespective of whether the President has actually seen a case or not, every order or sanction of the Union Government is expressed to have been made by the President.

Membership of Parliament is not a precondition to the appointment of person as minister but he must get elected within six months if he is to continue to hold his office. The Council of Ministers is made up of three classes of Ministers:

(a) senior ministers who are members of an informal body called the Cabinet—these are known as Ministers of Cabinet rank or Cabinet Ministers;
(b) other ministers who are known as Ministers of State;
(c) Deputy Ministers.

It is the Cabinet which shapes and finally determines the policy of the Government and also takes decisions on important administrative questions. Ministers of Cabinet rank, of course, attend these meetings of the Cabinet. At such meetings a Minister of State or a Deputy Minister is called in when the Cabinet proceeds to discuss any matter assigned to him.

Organization of a Ministry

Various functions of governmental activities are distributed according to administrative convenience among different ministries. In other words, the administrative set-up of the Government of India is divided into Ministries.

A ministry ordinarily comprises two or more departments, a minister being in-charge of all of them. Sometimes two or more ministries are placed under the charge of one and the same minister. There are also certain departments which are not included in any ministry as such but which function as separate units, e.g., the Department of Atomic Energy. The following are a few examples of such departments:

Department of Iron and Steel Department of Mines and Fuel	Under Ministry of Steel, Mines and Fuel
Department of Education Department of Cultural Activities and Physical Education Department of Scientific Research and Technical Education	Under Ministry of Education, Human Resources and Development
Department of Parliamentary Affairs	Under Parliamentary Affairs Ministry

The Union Secretariat

The business of the Government of India is primarily transacted in the Union or Central Secretariat.* The Union Secretariat consists of the several ministries and of some departments such as the Atomic Energy Department.

*Note: The President's Secretariat also deals with certain Union subjects but these subjects are mostly concerned with the President's staff, his budget, ceremonial functions, his tours and the like. Some work relating to the military is also carried out by the Military Secretary to the President.

A ministry/department is an organizational unit consisting of a Secretary to Government in the concerned ministry/ department with a part of the Central Secretariat under his administrative control. While the political head of a ministry is a minister, the administrative head is the Secretary to the

Government of India in the concerned Ministry. His principal function is to advise the minister on all matters of policy and administration arising in the ministry. He also passes final orders in ordinary cases (mostly of a routine nature) and/or other such cases as may be assigned to him by any general or special orders of the Minister.

The organization and efficiency of the ministry is, of course, primarily a responsibility of the Minister, in-charge but, speaking broadly, the Secretary acts as the coordinator of all activities of the ministry and is accountable for the advice given to the Minister in all matters as well as for ensuring the implementation of the decisions of the minister and those of the Council of Ministers in matters concerning his ministry.

To cope with the volume of work in a ministry, some wings are established within it, each under the charge of a Joint Secretary. In some cases, there is a Special Secretary/Additional Secretary also, who too has a wing or wings assigned to him. In such cases, the Special or Additional Secretary or Joint Secretary, as the case may be, is vested with a large measure of independent action (subject, of course, to ministerial control) but on the whole his responsibility and functioning is subject to the Secretary's overall general supervision.

For the more convenient disposal of business, the ministry is divided into divisions, branches and sections, the lowest unit being the Section. A section is in the immediate charge of a Section Officer and consists of the required number of clerical staff, e.g., assistants, upper and lower division clerks, typists, diarists, etc. Two or more sections form a branch which is normally under the charge of an Under Secretary. Then there is the division which comprises a couple of branches and is normally under the charge of a Deputy Secretary.

A Deputy Secretary or Under Secretary transacts certain matters directly with the Minister but the Secretary keeps himself informed of such cases by seeing the relevant file on its return from the Minister, whereafter the file passed down to the officer concerned for action on the orders passed. Apart from such cases all proposals involving policy matters or important administrative questions have to be routed through the Joint Secretary or the Secretary or both.

Secretariat Procedure

Communications addressed to a Ministry/Department are received in the Central Registry which distributes them to the sections concerned. On receipt in the section, the diarist submits them to the Section Officer who, after going through them, classifies the same into two categories:

(i) Primary, that is initial receipts regarding original or new items of work, and

(ii) Subsidiary, that is receipts emanating in connection with prime receipts in the course of interim consultations or references.

The primary receipts are further subdivided into two categories, viz.:

(a) Those requiring elaborate examination or prolonged consultations and not expected to be disposed of within a month, and

(b) Others.

After such classification the Section Officer marks them to the dealing assistants. Those receipts which are of a difficult nature or present any special features requiring his personal attention are dealt with by the Section Officer himself, or special instructions are given by him to the dealing assistant.

The urgent communications out of the daily receipts are marked by Section Officer to higher officers for any orders considered necessary at the initial stage itself. After these operations, the receipts come back to the diarist who (registers) them and passes them to the marked assistants.

Now comes the main function in the disposal of a receipt. The assistant gets out the relevant file, if one already exists, or in non-exists, he opens a new file. He then consults indices, file registers, sectional notebook of important decisions maintained in the section and other relevant books, enactments, rules, etc. with the aid of these, he prepares a note and submits the file to the Section Officer. The latter scrutinises the note, adds his own comments or suggestions, if any, and submits the case to the Branch Officer (Under Secretary). On his own responsibility the Under Secretary disposes of as many cases as possible. For the rest, he obtains the orders of the Deputy Secretary or a higher officer according to the complexity of the matter.

As a general proposition, the Deputy Secretary is vested with some delegated powers and disposes of certain types of cases himself. The more important ones are submitted by him to the Additional Secretary/ Joint Secretary or Secretary according to the standing distribution of work. It is only in cases involving policy decisions or important administrative matters that they are submitted to the latter officers.

Finally, the Additional/Joint Secretary or Secretary, in his turn submits the more important cases to the Minister and in doing so he prepares a self-contained summary of the case. In most such cases the Minister disposes of the file himself by passing the final orders. Only a few are referred by him to the Council of Ministers with the prior approval of the Prime Minister. Rules exist as to the classes of cases which require the orders of the Council of Ministers with the residuary rule giving discretion to the Prime Minister to refer any other cases to the Council, the Minister too may, with Prime Minister's approval, refer any residuary case to the Council.

Rules of Business

A detailed description of the procedure for the transaction of business in the ministries is laid down in the Rules of Business, framed by the President under Article 77(3) of the Constitution. These rules are of a secret nature and are meant for use only in the Central Secretariat.

Cabinet Secretariat

Herein, is done the work connected with the meetings of the Cabinet, maintenance of records of the decisions of the Cabinet and its Committees. There are several other items also, such as Cabinet Coordination, Statistical Organization, etc.

The Prime Minister is the political head of the Cabinet Secretariat, which has its own Secretary designated as Secretary to the Cabinet. The Cabinet Secretariat comprises:

(i) Main Secretariat;
(ii) Organization and Methods (O & M) Division;
(iii) Military Wing;
(iv) Economic Wing.

There is then the Attached Offices, namely the Central Statistical Organization which was created in 1961. Its functions are broad-based in the field of statistics.

Planning Commission

As supplemental to the Ministries/Departments of the Government of India, there is the Planning Commission headed by the Prime Minister as Chairman. It was set up in 1950 with a view to making the country self-sufficient, both in matters regarding agriculture and industry which had earlier been emphasised by the Government of India soon after the attainment of independence in the Industrial Policy Resolution of April 1948. The Commission formulates programmes of development and sees to their execution. Since its inception, it has been making 5-year plans and after due approval, ensuring their execution both in the Central field and in the States.

Attached Offices

Under various ministries there are Attached Offices which are responsible for providing executive directions required in the implementation of policies, plans and programmes laid down by the Ministry to which they are attached. Example of some of the Attached Offices are given below:

Attached Offices	*Ministry to which attached*
Union Public Service Commission Central Intelligence Bureau Commissioner for Scheduled Castes and Scheduled Tribes Special Police Establishment	Ministry of Home Affairs
Office of the Chief Controller of Exports Office of the Salt Commissioner	Ministry of Commerce and Industry
Directorate of Marketing and Inspection Directorate of Economics and Statistics	Ministry of Food and Agriculture

Heads of Departments and Subordinate Offices

These function principally as field establishments responsible for detailed execution of the projects, decisions, etc. They usually function under the direction of an Attached Office or in cases where the volume of executive direction is inconsiderable directly under a ministry. The following table illustrates the position:

Ministry	*Attached Office*	*Head of Department of Subordinate Office*
Ministry of Transport and Communication	Directorate General Posts and Telegraphs	Directors of Posts and Telegraphs of various circles
Ministry of Finance	Office of National Savings Commissioner	Regional National Savings Officers in the States
Ministry of Information and Broadcasting	Directorate General All India Radio	Station Directors of various Broadcasting Stations
	Press Information Bureau	Information Officers of the Bureau in State Capitals

REFERENCE

1. Morley, as a member of the Asouith Cabinet before the First World War.

THREE

ORGANIZATION OF STATE GOVERNMENTS

The following administrative structure chart shows at a glance the administrative set-up of the State Government:

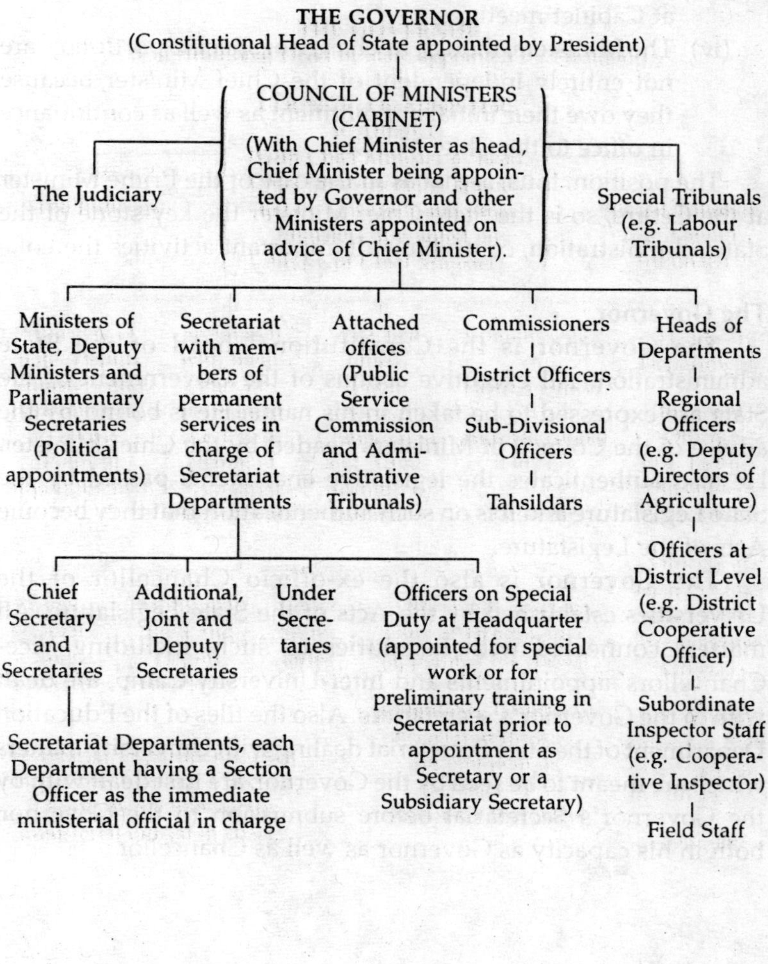

With reference to the above chart certain basic points may be stated:

(i) Although the Governor is the head of the State, the power of administration virtually vests in the Cabinet.

(ii) The Chief Minister as the head of the Cabinet possesses an over-riding power in all matters.

(iii) The Chief Secretary also plays a vital role in State affairs. He controls the Secretariat, the headquarter organization of administration and is directly responsible to the Chief Minister. He is also the head of the services in the State. Additionally, being a senior administrative officer with wide experience, his advice carries special weight. As Secretary to the Cabinet he also influences the deliberations at Cabinet meetings.

(iv) The Ministers, though in-change of specific portfolios, are not entirely independent of the Chief Minister because they owe their initial appointment as well as continuance in office to the Chief Minister.

The position, thus, is that as in the case of the Prime Minister at the Centre, so is the State Chief Minister the key-stone of the State administration, controlling all important activities thereof.

The Governor

The Governor is the Constitutional head of the State administration. All executive actions of the Government of the State are expressed to be taken in his name. He is bound by the advice of the Council of Ministers headed by the Chief Minister. He also authenticates the legislative enactments passed by the State Legislature and it is on such authentication that they become Acts of the Legislature.

The Governor is also the ex-officio Chancellor of the Universities established by the Acts of the State Legislature. All matters connected with his duties as such, including Vice-Chancellors' appointments and Inter-University Camp, are dealt with in the Governor's secretariate. Also the files of the Education Department of the State Secretariat dealing with University matters which are meant to be seen by the Governor, are first dealt with by the Governor's Secretariat before submission to the Governor, both in his capacity as Governor as well as Chancellor.

The Governor of the State is not a person elected to his office and in this respect the office of the Governor differs from the office of the President of the Union, who is elected by an electoral college provided for in the Constitution. The Governor is appointed by the President, who, in this matter acts on the advice of the Union Cabinet. The Governor holds office at the pleasure of the President and subject to it he holds it for five years.

The Governor, as the Constitutional head of the State, acts on the advice of his ministers. The Constitution authorises him to exercise his functions in certain matters using his own discretion (i.e., he can act otherwise rather than in accordance with the advice of his Ministers) but so far as Uttar Pradesh is concerned, there are no such matters reserved for the discretionary powers of the Governor. (It is only the Governor of Assam who has been invested by the Constitution with certain discretionary power in respect of the tribal area in that State.)

The Governor has a moderate-sized secretarial staff under the charge of the Secretary to the Governor. This staff deals with the following principal items:

- (i) Work which comes to the Governor in his capacity as Chancellor of each of the Universities in the State.
- (ii) Work connected with numerous semi-official and private institutions with which the Governor and his wife are associated.
- (iii) Tours, engagements and social functions held or attended by the Governor, cultural activities of the Governor and his wife.
- (iv) Visits of the President, Prime Minister and other VIPs.
- (v) Control of the money allotted for the Governor and the Government House under the Constitution and the rules made by the President, thereunder.

The Governor's Secretariat thus, in addition to its own functions as an administrative unit, in-charge of the budget relating to the Governor, the Secretariat Staff and the Raj Bhawan, has to operate as a corporate office. The Governor's Secretariat is not concerned with the papers submitted to the Governor by the ministers relating to certain matters. These are laid before him directly without the intervention of any member of his staff.

The Cabinet or Council of Ministers

The Chief Minister, under the Constitution, is the head of the Cabinet, formally known as Council of Ministers. He is appointed by the Governor and the other ministers are appointed by the Governor on the advice of the Chief Minister. The Chief Minister is chosen by the Governor from the political party commanding a majority in the Legislative Assembly of the State. Under the Constitution, the Council of Ministers owes collective responsibility to the Legislative Assembly. The collective responsibility is not to the 'Legislature', i.e., the Legislative Assembly, which is the Lower House and the Legislative Council which is the Upper House. It is only the Assembly to which the Council of Ministers is responsible.

The Chief Minister presides at the meetings of the Cabinet. The business of the Government including the business of the Cabinet is transacted under statutory rules framed under the Constitution. These rules are entitled the 'The Rules of Business'.

Position Under President's Rule

The Council of Ministers ceases to exist when the President assumes to himself the functions of the State Government. This is permissible when the President is satisfied that a situation has arisen in which the administration of the State cannot be carried on in accordance with the provisions of the Constitution relating to the administration of States including provisions for the formation of the Council of Ministers. Such assumption is done by the issuance of a proclamation by the President in which the necessary incidental and consequential provisions are also made for carrying out the administration of the State and the making of Laws.

Such a proclamation unless earlier revoked, remains in full operation initially for six months provided it is, meanwhile, approved by Parliament. It can, however, be continued for a total period of one year, subject to Parliament's periodical approval at interval of six months or so.

When the President thus assumes the function of the State Government, the administration is carried on personally by the Governor subject to the superintendence, direction and control of the Union Government. To assist the Governor in this task, a panel of Advisers consisting of senior members of the Civil Administrative Cadre (IAS) is appointed. A group of departments of the secretariat is assigned to each adviser who then becomes responsible for the proper functioning of those departments. Periodic meetings of the Advisers, presided over by the Governor, take place to consider the matters of policy and important administrative problems.

The order of the State Government issued during this proclamation period are issued in the name of the Governor as in normal time with certain exceptions. Such a proclamation is generally issued when there is no single political party commanding a majority in the Legislative Assembly which can form the government. Alternatively, there can be a combination of certain political parties which can successfully form a coalition government if they collectively command a majority in the assembly. If that too is not possible, there would be no option but to enforce the Presidential rule.

The President's rule also comes into play if the majority party in the assembly does not, for any reason, accept the responsibility for forming the government and there is no combination of the remaining parties which can command a majority in the assembly to be able to form the government. The same result follows when the majority party having formed the government in the beginning is unwilling at a later stage to carry on the government for any reason and resigns in consequence.

For a clearer appreciation of the position about the President's rule, extracts from the proclamation of the President issued on June 13, 1973 are reproduced below. It was issued in consequence of the resignation of Kamlapati Tripathi's Congress Party ministry in Uttar Pradesh which though enjoyed a comfortable majority in the assembly declined to continue in office in consequence of the serious revolt of the Pradeshik Armed Constabulary (P.A.C.) and the disastrous incidents caused in the university by the students in collaboration with the revolting members of the P.A.C. who had earlier been posted in the Lucknow University campus to prevent the students from causing disturbance.

Proclamation

This was issued by Government of India, Home Ministry's Notification No. G.S.R. 316(E) dated 13-6-1973, extracts from it are as follows:

"The following proclamation by the President is published for general information :

Whereas I, V.V. Giri, President of India, have received a report from the Government of the State of Uttar Pradesh and after considering the report and other information received by me, I am satisfied that a situation has arisen in which the government of that State cannot be carried on in accordance with the provisions of the Constitution of India (hereafter referred to as 'the Constitution').

Now, therefore, in exercise of the powers conferred by Article 356 of the Constitution and of all other powers enabling me in that behalf I hereby proclaim that, I :

(a) assume to myself as President of India, all functions of the government of the said State and all powers vested in or exercisable by the Governor of that State:

(b) declare that the powers of the Legislature of that State shall be exercisable by or under the authority of Parliament; and

(c) make the following incidental and consequential provisions which appear to me to be necessary or desirable for giving effect to the objects of this proclamation namely:

(i) in the exercise of the functions and powers assumed to myself by virtue of clause (a) of the proclamation as aforesaid, it shall be lawful for me as President of India to act to such extent as I think fit through the Governor of the said State;

(ii) the operation of the following provisions of the Constitution in relation to that State is hereby suspended, namely-

(iii) any reference in the Constitution to the Governor in relation to the said State shall be construed as a reference to the President.......

Provided that nothing, herein shall prevent the President from acting under sub-clause (i) of this clause to such extent as he thinks fit through the Governor of the said State;

(iv) x x x

New Delhi, Sd/- V.V. Giri
Dated the 13th June, 1973 President
New Delhi Sd/- Ashok Sen
Dated the 13th June 1973 Special Secretary"

Simultaneous with the issuance of the above Proclamation, the President passed the following order :

"In pursuance of sub-clause (i) of clause (c) of the Proclamation issued on this 13th day of June, 1973, by me under Article 356 of the Constitution of India, I hereby direct that all the functions of the Government of the State of Uttar Pradesh and all the powers vested in or exercisable by the Governor of that State under the Constitution or under any law in force in that State, which have been assumed by the President by virtue of clause (a) of the said Proclamation, shall, subject to the superintendence direction and control of the President, be exercisable also by the Governor of the said State.

New Delhi Sd/- V.V. Giri
Dated the 13th June, 1973 President"

Upon the promulgation of the above proclamation the resignation of the Council of Ministers headed by Pandit Kamlapati Tripathi, Chief Minister, became effective from the date of proclamation, that is 13-6-1973. A notification dated 14-3-73 of the U.P. Government to this effect was accordingly published.

As will be observed from the foregoing documents the administration of the State during President's rule is carried on:

(a) by the President on the advice of the Union Council of Ministers, and

(b) by the Governor acting as the agent of the President.

It is, therefore, within the jurisdiction of the President in appropriate matters to issue orders or sanctions on the advice of the Union Ministry notwithstanding the fact that in day-to-day affairs, the powers to make decisions has been entrusted by the President to the Governor. Accordingly, when an order or sanction is issued from the Government of India, it is expressed to be made in the name of the President. Likewise, when it is issued from the State Secretariat, it is expressed to have been made by the Governor.

The Secretariat

The Secretariat is a large office located in the capital town, the headquarter of the State Government. It is through this office that the government works as the central controlling authority in the State. By the government here is meant the Governor and his Ministers working as a composite entity. The Secretariat is the nerve centre of the government and has its own importance. The understanding of the practical working of the Secretariat is thus of paramount importance to those administrative officers who have no personal experience of having worked in it.

Attached Offices

The offices of the Public Service Commission and the Administrative Tribunal are usually known as attached offices.

Public Service Commission

The State Public Service Commission is an important body in the affairs of the State. It is responsible for appointments not only to the administrative services under the Governor's rule making control but also in respect of all State services and other important services. The interests of the members of these services are also committed to its charge in respect of disciplinary matters and the like. (The subject has accordingly been dealt with independently in Chapter 32 entitled "Public Service Commission".)

Administrative Tribunal

This has been dealt with in Chapter 3 Vigilance Commission, Vigilance Establishment and Administrative Tribunal.

Accountant General's Office

The Accountant General's Office is neither under the control of the State Government nor are its expenses met from the State budget. It is controlled by the Comptroller and Auditor General of India and funds for its working are provided by the Central

Government. This is because the subject of "Audit of the accounts of the Union and of States is a Central subject and, therefore, the financial responsibility for maintaining the audit organization is of the Central Government. The Accountant General is a part of this organization of which the head is the Comptroller and Auditor General of India."

Nevertheless, the Accountant General is in charge of the accounts of the State Government and no money can be issued out of the State funds without the formal authority conveyed by him to the Treasury Officers who either pay money out of the treasuries (e.g. pensions of small amounts) or pass bills for actual payment by various branches of the State Bank of India. An exception to the above rule is that the Finance Department of the State Government may in emergent and exceptional cases authorise payment without the formal authority of the Accountant General.

The Accountant General is also the authority in respect of receipts and disbursements of the State Government. In this capacity he acts as the agent of the Comptroller and Auditor General of India who is the paramount and independent audit authority for the whole of India including the Union Government.

Heads of Departments, Principal Heads of Offices and Heads of Offices

These are senior officers who are in overall charge of the execution of the projects and the execution and /or actual administration of specific services. These Heads of Departments are in charge of development departments, e.g., the Irrigation Department, the Agriculture Department, the Industries Department which deal with the execution of new projects and the administration and running projects. Then there are Heads of Departments who are in charge of purely executive departments, e.g., the Police Department which is under the charge of the Inspector General of Police, or the Prisons Department which is under the Inspector General of Prisons. Then there are certain Heads of Departments who are concerned with the collection of taxes and the administration of taxation, e.g. the Board of Revenue, the Land Reforms Commissioner, which are concerned with the collection of taxes on land and the administration of the law relating to land tenancy. There is then the Entertainment and Betting Tax Commissioner who is concerned with the collection of entertainment and betting taxes and the administration of the law relating thereto.

The funds voted by the Legislature are placed at the disposal of each Head of Department—it is only in respect of certain specified matters that some earmarked funds are retained at the disposal of the Minister-in-charge. The Head of Department is responsible for the proper utilisation of the funds so placed at his disposal and to render an account therefore to the Accountant General and through him to the Public Accounts Committee and the Legislature.

The running schemes are administered according to the pattern which had, in the past, received government's sanction. The new schemes are first considered by the government either of their own accord or on reference made by Heads of Departments and provision as considered necessary is made in the budget. After the budget has been passed, the Heads of Departments are directed to carry out the schemes according to the design formulated by government and approved by the Legislature at the time of the budget. In conveying this authorisation, the Head of Department is informed about the number of posts sanctioned for the scheme with their scales of pay and the other funds available to him for the execution of the scheme.

Each Head of Department has under him regional officers and officers in charge of districts. Thus, in each district there is a representative of the Heads of Departments and supervision of a specified number of districts is done by a regional officer. For instance, in the Agriculture Department there are, under the Director of Agriculture, Deputy Directors of Agriculture in charge of agriculture regions and under them there are District Agriculture Officers. Nevertheless the overall superintendence of the departmental activities vests in the Head of Department alone who is answerable to the government at the headquarter. The Head of Department has no access to Secretariat files. He, however, has free access to the minister-in charge of his department and the Chief Minister.

The Head of Department has his separate office at the

headquarter of the government but there are a few exceptions, for instance the main office of the Director of Education is located not at Lucknow but at Allahabad. The Director has, however, a camp office at Lucknow, where he also resides. Similarly, the main office of the Board of Revenue and that of the Director General of Police are at Allahabad.

Being in charge of executive functions, the Head of Department has to do extensive touring to see that the departmental activities spread over the whole State, are being properly looked after by regional and field officers.

The office of the Head of Department is divided into sections each under the charge of a Head Clerk who supervises the work of other clerks. There are a few officers attached to the office who have specific subjects allotted to them with which they deal under the general control of the Head of Department. There is also a Personal Assistant of gazetted rank who looks after establishment matters of the main office and is in charge of other specified matters.

The procedure of work in these offices is not so elaborate as in the secretariat. No extensive noting in files is done and in many cases drafts with fair copies are prepared by the clerks without discussing the matter in office note. One of the main functions of the office is the transmission of government orders, etc. to subordinate offices with such supplementary or detailed instructions as may be called for. The Head of Department also disposes of references from subordinate officers to the extent of the powers delegated to him; in others he seeks orders of the government by making formal references.

Every now and then information about the activities of the department or of happenings at the district level is required by the government for answering questions in the Legislature. The Head of Department acts as the coordinating officer for the purpose of collecting and consolidating the information before its transmission to government with the observations.

Principal Heads of Offices

In addition to Heads of Departments there are certain quasi-heads of departments, that is to say those who, though not formally designated as Head of Department, nevertheless stand on practically the same footings as Heads of Departments. Examples are the Superintendent, Printing and Stationery; the Examiner, Local Fund Accounts; The Chief Audit Officer, Panchayat and Co-operative Societies. These officers are called Principal Heads of Offices. The financial and administrative provisions applicable to Heads of Departments apply *mutatis mutandis* to Principal Heads of Office.

There are then certain other senior officers who wield considerable administrative powers but who have no regular department under their charge, for instance Commissioner of Divisions. These officers are also known as Principal Heads of Offices.

Heads of Offices

The unit of administration is the district and each department has its representative in each district*. Thus the representative of Government for General Administration in the district is the District Officer. Similarly, the District Inspector of Schools represents the Education Department in the district, the Superintendent of Police, the Police Department and so on.

As a general proposition the officer in charge of an administrative unit is the Head of Office irrespective of the fact whether the geophysical limit of the unit is a revenue district or a departmental division. Thus, the District Officer is the Head of Office, so also the Executive Engineer.

The above is a broad definition of Head of Office. There may be other officers too who may be Head of Offices though not falling within the above description.

Divisional Commissioners and other Regional Officers

In the sphere of general administration, there is no Head of Department. The subject is controlled directly by the headquarter of the government, that is the Secretariat and the Chief Secretary is the officer who deals with it under the direction of the Chief

Note: *There are a few exceptions to this general rule, for example, in the Public Works Department and Irrigation Department, the unit administration is not a district but a P.W.D. or Irrigation Division (as distinguished from a Revenue Division under a Commissioner). The officer in charge of this division is the Executive Engineer.

Minister. The secretariat departments principally concerned are the General Administration Department, the Confidential Department and the Appointments Departments, all in the branch of the Chief Secretary.

Commissioners

The District Officers are the immediate officers responsible for this. They are supervised by the Commissioners of the divisions who are the Regional Officers for general administration. The Commissioners have also many functions to perform in connection with the affairs of local bodies. The enactments connected therewith contain the necessary provisions about this. In each division there is an Additional Commissioner who hears appeals in land tenure cases and in other matters of a similar nature.

Regional Officers

For regular departments there are Regional Officers under the Head of Department concerned. In some cases the regions of these officers are same as the revenue divisions under Commissioner; in others, the departments have their own departmental regions. These regions are also known as circles. For instance, there are Regional Deputy Directors of Education, Superintending Engineers of the Irrigation Department in charge of Irrigation Circles. In some cases the region is called 'Range' as in the Police organization.

The functions of the Regional Officers are mostly supervisory, as in the case of Divisional Commissioners. The Regional Officers are responsible to the Heads of Departments who control them from headquarters.

District Administration

District administration should be taken as meaning the general administration of the district which is the administrative unit of the State Government. This 'general administration' includes law and order and the magistracy, as also some planning work which has an important place in the present welfare State. The District Officer is in charge of this 'general administration'.

The District Officer (known as District Magistrate) is also, in an informal capacity, concerned with the general well-being and progress of his district although he does not exercise any direct control over the activities of the various nation-building departments or their representatives in the district. For instance, though he is not directly concerned with the subject of irrigation which is the immediate concern of the Executive Engineer, still the District Officer comes into the picture either through the committees or in some other manner regarding irrigation projects in the district. In this way he is an officer who is concerned, though indirectly, with the overall activities in his district. Thus the District Officer is, so to say, an all-embracing officer whose advice is sought in matters which are directly under the charge of officers of other departments. To illustrate the point, though the District Officer is not directly concerned with the educational activities in the district, for which there is the District Inspector of Schools, nevertheless he has a role in situations arising from mass activities of students. In short, he represents the government in his district.

In performing such duties, which in many cases are of an unwritten nature, the District Officer has to bring his tact and personality to bear upon the matters. His administrative capability enables him to coordinate the activities to ensure their smooth working in liaison with other departmental officers stationed in the district. In regard to development work in the district, the District Officer has been formally given some controlling authority over the local officers of the development departments, e.g., the District Cooperative Officer, the District Agriculture Officer, the District Planning Officer the last one being also designated as Additional District Officer (Planning). Through this officer, the District Magistrate coordinate the development activities.

There is also the District Supply Officer who looks after the supply of controlled commodities and in some districts he also carries on the work of allotment of houses, shop, etc. control over him vests in the District Officer. There is also the Rent Control and Eviction Officer.

There is then the Treasury Officer who remains in immediate charge of the district treasury and who exercises supervision over receipts and who authorises various payments, e.g. salaries, pensions, grants, contingent bills, payment to contractors, all through the State Bank of India on bills drawn by drawing and disbursing officers. The overall supervisory control over the treasury, however, vests in the District Officer (District Magistrate).

Tehsils

In various tehsils of the district there is the Tehsildar who is in charge of the tehsil sub-treasury as sub-treasury officer. At the same time he carries on executive functions, the most important of which are the timely collection of land dues and the maintenance of land records. He also exercises some magisterial powers of a petty nature.

In addition, there are generally a few extra officers (apart from the sub-divisional officer and the treasury officer) attached to the District Officer, who control and supervise various branches of the District Office such as work relating to land records, State exercise, collections, payment to some dependable departments, relief grants, compensations, etc. Compulsory acquisition of land for public purpose under the Land Acquisition Act is also done through the District Officer who has under him for this purpose a District Acquisition Officer, either part-time or full-time depending upon the volume of work.

The District Officer is, in almost all matters, directly answerable to government for the matters under his charge. It is only in certain statutory functions and a few others that the District Officer works under the direct control of the Divisional Commissioner, e.g., functions connected with local bodies.

District Superintendent of Police

In a State there are District Officers,(D.Ms) one each for each of the districts. To assist the District Magistrate in his law and order functions there is the District Superintendent of Police. This officer works in collaboration with the District Magistrate in the conduct of prosecutions and the investigation of crimes. Departmentally, he is responsible to the Inspector-General of Police through the Deputy Inspector General of Police.

In a few of the bigger districts there are Additional District Officers to relieve the District Officers of the large volume of their routine duties. Under the scheme for the separation of the executive and judicial functions there are also in certain districts Additional

District Magistrates (Judicial) who deal with judicial cases and do no executive work. There are also Additional District Magistrates (Planning) who are in charge of the development activities in the district. For instance, they supervise the work of Block Development Officers (BDOs).

Sub-Divisional Officer

For the purpose of general administration each district is sub-divided into sub-divisions or tehsils and in charge of each sub-division is a Sub-divisional Officer, (S.D.M.) who is a member of the State Civil Service (Executive Branch). These Sub-divisional Officers possess revenue powers also and try judicial cases pertaining to land revenue, land tenancy and disputes concerning agricultural land under the relevant land laws. Appeals against their judgements are heard by the Additional Commissioners and through them by the Board of Revenue.

Executive Magistrate

Under the scheme of separation of the judiciary from the executive, these officers who are treated as Executive Magistrates do not deal with criminal cases except with minor offences. In Uttar Pradesh, they deal primarily with land tenure cases that is, case under the U.P. Zamindari Abolition and Land Reforms Act (and allied Acts), U.P. Land Revenue Act. In addition they deal with the following miscellaneous items:

(a) cases under the preventive provisions of the Criminal Procedure Code,
(b) cases under miscellaneous local and special Acts, e.g. Arms Act, Excise Act, Prevention of Food Adulteration Act, Gambling Act, Essential Commodities Act, and
(c) conduct of identification-proceeding recordings, of dying declarations, confessions, etc.

The regular criminal trial work is entrusted to Munsif Magistrates and officers of the State Judicial Service which includes posts of Additional District Magistrate (Judicial) and Judicial Officer or Judicial Magistrate. Serious cases are, however, heard by Sessions Judge and District Judges. In U.P. since 1967, no further recruitment is, however, being made to the posts of Judicial Officer whose place is now being gradually taken by Munsif Magistrates. In this way the cadre of Judicial Officers will disappear in course of time and ultimately criminal cases under the I.P.C. at the magisterial level will all come to be dealt with by Munsif Magistrates who will have only criminal judicial work to perform and no executive work.

The Judiciary

The State judiciary consists of the High Court and the subordinate courts, i.e., District Judges and other officers of the subordinate judiciary. The State judiciary is independent of the executive (Government)—Judges of the High Court being appointed by the President in accordance with a special unpublished procedure. Appointment and promotion of District Judges is made by the Government in consultation with the High Court. Appointment of other officers to the Judicial Service of the State is made by the Government in accordance with rules after consultation with the Public Service Commission and with the High Court. Control over district courts and courts subordinate thereto, includes the posting and promotion, the grant of leave to persons belonging to the Judicial Service and holding any post inferior to the post of District Judge, is vested in the High Court. It is in this manner that it has been secured that the judiciary shall be independent of the executive (Government). The composition of Judiciary is given in the following chart.

This chart shows the administrative structure at a glance of the Judiciary of the State Government:

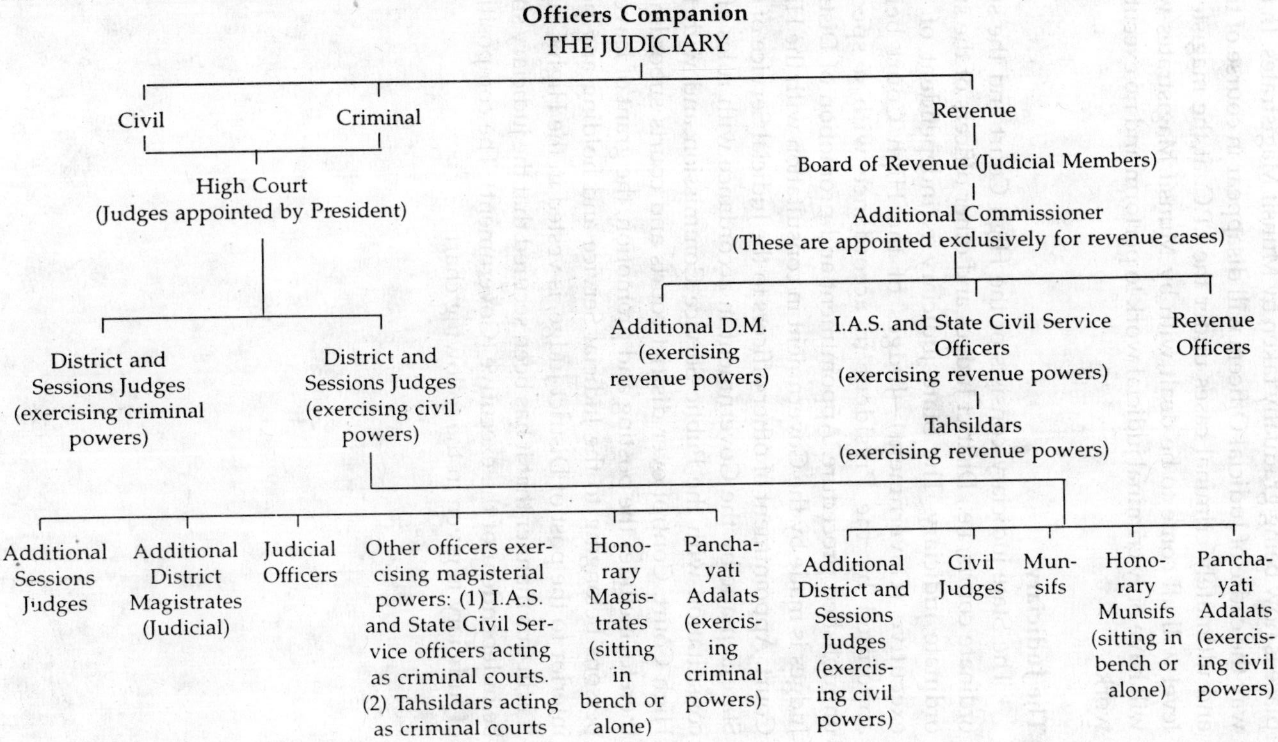

FOUR

MANAGEMENT IN GOVERNMENT

Unfortunately, in the public sector, the top management has not adapted to the changed conditions. It remains bogged in rules and procedures, regulation and control and distrust and suspicions. It has rarely been given adequate and consistent attention to the building of an appropriate culture of organization. Strategies and plans are prepared in isolation from employees and organization culture. For too long, the hard quantitative management techniques have been accentuated over supposedly soft people skill. The top management has focused on the short-term orientation of their organization, e.g., preoccupation with monthly, quarterly and annual target achievements rob long-term development needs and prevents the creation of or exploitation of opportunities. The management can only create excellence when it replaces short-term needs with long-term development and well-being. The top management must find a way to balance short-term with long-term expectations.

No genuine consistent approach to people orientation has been made by the top management in public sector. Most of the organizations of the public sector are governed by rules that assume the average worker to be dishonest, incompetent and never-do-good, just itching to botch the task. This kind of environment can never create efficiency and excellence. People will respond well to being treated as grown-ups, honest and trustworthy.

Lip-service Disaster

Genuine people orientation is in marked contrast to the two major alternatives, all too often seen in the organizations: the lip-service disaster and the gimmicks disaster. The lip-service management, having said that people are important, it does not pay much attention to the people. Sometimes new programmes like MBO Summary assessment or quality circles are tried when it becomes faddish. But each is soon rejected or bureaucratised. The failing is often attributed to a lack of employees' goodwill. Seldom is it attributed to a lack of persistence and true caring on the part of the management.

That leads to the second problem: gimmicks trap. Slogans like— "I trust you, you trust me", "file, smile and go" have failed to produce the desired response and results. These ideas are good but in practice they simply serve as smoke-screens, while the management continues to get away with not doing its job of meaningful people involvement.

Excessive Structuring

Another problem bedevilling in public sector is excessive structuring and layering. This has widened the gulf between the management and the people. It is done primarily to make member of place for a larger higher posts, though shown as a measure of control. Extra levels of management mainly create distracting work for others to justify their own existence. Everyone appears busy but in reality it is simple management feather-bedding.

Decentralisation

To secure people's involvement and willing voluntary co-operation it is necessary to have less structuring and layering and keep the areas of work and decisions divided in small units. Small is productive. The point for smallness is that it induces manageability and above all commitment. In small, one central discipline prevail. Even in organisations that employ hundreds of thousands of people the divisions are small enough, or if there are other ways of simulating autonomy, the individual still counts and can stand out. There is no other way an individual can stick out unless the size of units is of human scale.

Small government offices in mofussil areas are more productive. In large metropolitan offices there is less of discipline and punctuality, more absenteeism, distractions, unrest and costly dissatisfaction. Along with bigness comes complexity and most big organizations respond to complexity in kind by designing complex systems and structures. They then line up more staff to keep track of all this complexity and that is where the mistake begins. If a manager can control all aspects of his division it will run a lot better. It would be worthwhile to find ways of dividing public sector into small autonomous divisions.

Recent events in some communist countries have shown that there is no alternative to people's orientation in management of government. There is a need for starting a genuine *people involvement programme* and execute it sincerely and consistently.

THE GOOD ADMINISTRATOR

Chakravarti Rajagopalachari, the outstanding statesman, seasoned administrator and the last Governor-General of independent India, had given an analytical description of a good administrator in a talk delivered on August 14, 1955 under 'Sardar Vallabh Bhai Patel Lectures' series. The veteran statesman posed the question, "what are the requirements we should demand in a good administrator?" and then proceeded to suggest the following traits for a good administrator:

Character Alone not the Decisive Factor

Character is, of course, a basic requirement but it alone is not all-sufficient. A very good man may not at all be fit to be entrusted with administrative responsibility in the civil business of the State, even as it is obviously the case in the conduct of a military operation. We know of persons of undoubted good character who have failed as administrators. To the above proposition the learned statesman has added a word of caution by saying that he should not be taken to mean that character is to be relegated to the background. True, it alone is not enough but without it, nothing else will avail. Character is as important for administrators at every level, from the Chief Secretary down to the last grade servant, as sunlight is to every form of life.

Experts not Administrators

Experts cannot govern nor can they be safely allowed to govern, though they may wish and, if permitted, be able to dominate. In administrative key positions, the special technical equipment that comes into play in their departments is not essential requirement. For example, the man responsible for fine and rapid development of the electricity-system in Madras State (when Rajagopalachari was the Chief Minister there) was not an electrician. An electrical engineer could not have done it. To achieve work of public interest we need practical will.

Right Judgement and Quick Decision

What is essential at the top is the capacity to judge what is relevant advice and decide promptly and rightly in administrative matters. Judicial offices are not the only places where the capacity to judge is essential. In small as well as great affairs he proves to be a good administrator who has this talent for right judgement and quick decision. Sagacity and imagination are the terms that describe the talent required for judging right. This quality is largely inborn, but early training can develop it. If there be seeds of inborn talent, experience also nourishes and enlarges them. There are some people who, though themselves are not able to judge matters, have the capacity to choose men possessing that ability. Such a person, holding a key administrative position, will be a good administrator if he makes use of others endowed with that capacity. He should not be one who is jealous of it in others and who prefers yes-men instead.

Hasty Decision no Substitute for Speedy Decision

Decisions should be speedy but not hasty. They should be arrived at after due consultation or discussion. The administrator should have the capacity to obtain the best out of his expert advisers and understand quickly what they say. He should hear out the opinions and views of all concerned before arriving at his own decision. But nothing should be put off for the reason that one is not able to make up his mind about it. It is also important that those who are in the employment in other capacities in the government department concerned and the people who are affected by the course of administration must know that, in policy matters as well as in daily administration, they cannot get clear and binding decisions without delay and procrastination.

Decision should be Unalterable

Barring rare exceptions a well-considered decision should be unalterable. All concerned should be made to feel that there will be no 'messing about', no modification and counter-order recalling, revising or modifying it.

In the affairs of the world when so many factors come into interplay, one particular decision is not the only right decision. But any firm decision is better than indecision which is another name for vacillation. What theoretically may be an imperfect decision becomes the right decision when people come to realise that it is an unalterable decision. Further, those implementing the decision should also feel sure that they will be supported through every difficulty and unpleasantness, that they will not be let down at the first hurdle under pressure from some powerful sources. For good administration this is most important. It explains the success of most administrators as well as the failure of others.

Timing of Decision

The proper moment is important. The good administrator should not only decide quickly but should have the sagacity to know when to do a particular thing. For this purpose he has to grasp many factors and to evaluate them with a view to eliminating those which do not count.

Capacity to Execute the Decision

A good administrator commands the loyalty of his staff by infusing in them confidence that he will stand by them, however difficult or unpleasant the execution may be. He will mix with his subordinates and makes them believe in his firmness and firmness on the issues arising.

A negative quality is bad temper which is no substitute for firmness. It leads to his being surrounded by worthless people who can put up with bad temper. The better men drop off from one who threatens to do things unreasonably. The departure of good men means getting flatterers instead. It is thus stating the obvious to say that good temper pays, ill temper does not.

A good administrator instils a sense of social purpose among his staff. His men should be able to see that the thing to be accomplished is to fulfill a laudable purpose, a service to society. Dr. Pul Appleby lists twelve qualifications which go to make a good administrator. Crucial among them is willingness to assume responsibility, even a positive eagerness for it. But his eagerness should be tempered by self-confidence, avoiding the pitfalls of inflated ambition. Then there should be courage, a readiness to take risks as opposed to playing safe.

Strong Bent for Action

Next, he must be a man with a strong bent of action. He must tirelessly pursue means of improving the administration, must be open to suggestions for improvement must be an initiator of new ideas. "The higher the position in the line of authority, the more general abilities required".

N.R. Pillai, one of the able Indian Civil Servants, has observed: "What manner of man is the new civil servant to be? He should, it is clear, possess the traditional service virtues—efficiency, integrity and loyalty, more specially to policies and institutions. But of one supposed virtue, that of neutralism in matters with a social or suspected political content, he must rid himself. It has long remained an unchallenged maxim that the perfect civil servant must be completely neutral from a political point of view and prove himself the loyalty and obedient instrument of whatever party is in power. If this means that the model civil servant should create a political vacuum in his thinking, it is a doctrine which must be discarded. Every citizen has the right to develop and hold his own political views. With this right there can be *no interference*. But it is the duty of all public servants, as it is of students, not to become political partisans or to engage in political activities.

"Fortunately, for us, the ideal of a welfare State is not in our country a controversial political issue; it is the goal laid down in the Constitution itself. Far from being the neutralist, the public servant of today, and still more of tomorrow, should be one rich in human sympathy and with a fully awakened social conscience. To his work he must bring not only competence but faith and fervour and a mind, receptive as well as constructive, able to see beyond the immediate difficulties, the opportunities that lie ahead."

No Political Leanings

We have then the observations of H.V.R. Iyengar, another distinguished member of the I.C.S.,(retired), dealing with the relations between ministers and administrative officers. "As the old guard disappears", he says, "future ministers may be men not merely without administrative experience but without the romantic halo of political suffering, and it is particularly important that for regulating relations between them and the permanent officials, sound conventions should have been established. The solution does not lie in purely structural devices, in any 'organization and methods' directives, but in a realignment of the mutual attitude of ministers and officials. Basically, this means that, while it is clearly understood that the ministers are the deciding authorities and that their decision must be given effect to, it is the right and duty of the officials frankly and fearlessly to advise: this means that such frankness is appreciated and encouraged rather than frowned upon and that, in general, both sides respect each other. This is putting it in very simple form, of course, for respect transcends the more recognition of sphere of authority; it extends to the field of character, which is another matter."

The same idea has been propounded by John Pliffner in these words: "The realization of the factor that politics and administration cannot always be separated and isolated, should not vitiate the basic soundness of a gentleman's agreement that one will not encroach upon the other in a meddlesome manner. The success to be attained in this direction will depend largely upon the extent to which party politics is kept out of administration. This will entail just as great an obligation for the administrative personnel to abstain from political controversy as for the politicians to keep hands off administration."

The Democratic Spirit

For a full-fledged democracy there are several requirements such as:

(a) A democratic constitution—democratic not in outward form but in its fullest scope and spirit.

(b) The political parties through whom the constitution is worked—both the party in power and the parties in opposition have to function in their organization, as pure democratic units. The party with a dictatorial sort of organization would not be able to bring to bear a true spirit of democracy if put in charge of political power.

(c) The electorate too should be democratic minded.

(d) Not the least important is the factor that the public service should have a democratic bearing and a democratic outlook to be able to serve democratic statesmen representing the party in power and deal properly with the parties in opposition.

Stabilizing Effect of Administrators

The dictum voiced long ago by U.S. President Abraham Lincoln that 'democracy means government of the people, for the people and by the people' is only symbolically true. In actual practice, however, it means government of the party commanding a majority of votes (seats) in the Legislature or Parliament and today most of politicians holding seats belong to power camps who capture votes through fear or fraud. Therefore, no party in power at a given time can expect to hold on for good. Sovereignty passes sooner or later from one party to another. Which means that it is transferred from persons with one set of ideology to those upholding a different and usually opposite ideology.

Accordingly, the continuity of the administration would be broken and a revolution would follow on each occasion when one political party is replaced by another if there is no suitable element in the administrative machinery which survives periodic changes. But there does exist such an element in the form of the administrative officers of the country. It is in this sense that they can be called the steel frame of the government, unremovable by the changing fortunes of political parties.

ADMINISTRATIVE PRINCIPLES

The object of administrative study is to rescue executive methods from the confusion and costliness of empirical experiment and set them upon foundations laid deep in stable principles.

WOODROW WILSON[1]

Reference is made to a few observations of Sir Malcolm (later Lord) Hailey, a former Governor of Uttar Pradesh, who had been a distinguished member of the I.C.S. and an administrator of the highest repute. He was speaking to the officers and staff of the U.P. Secretariat on the eve of his departure from U.P. on the conclusion of his term. In the course of his short speech Sir Malcolm paid a tribute to the efficiency of the Secretariats in India making a particular mention of the U.P. Secretariat. In that connection he added that the Secretariats in India recalled the corresponding offices in Britain.

These observations came at the end of his address which he had opened with the remark just to be mentioned and which is quite relevant to the present discussion. He said that governmental administration was a most delicate and exacting matter involving the reconciliation of mutually conflicting interests, the satisfaction of public demands which arise in constant succession, the control of elements opposed to the administration, the communal conflicts—to mention just a few examples of the problems that confront the administrator.

To Govern Well

To govern well, Sir Malcolm went on to say, was no easy task. It meant the interplay of many factors, often pulling in different directions' people—involved in a common task—with divergent ideas on what is right. There were than people at different stages of maturity, kinds of temperament, habits and practices. Public administration was thus a subtle matter. The successful administrator had, therefore, to be a person of the highest calibre, not in the mastery of rules, but in the principles of administration, in the understanding of human psychology, in the assessment of the effect of his actions on the governed, in his moral fibre and in a variety of other traits too numerous to enlist.

These observations are true in independent India as they were in Sir Malcolm Hailey's time. But while this is conceded, the question is whether there are any principles of administrative action and behaviour. There are, but they are too fluid to be encompassed within the framework of a literary article or a scientific discourse. All that is possible is to indicate certain broad features of the subject by referring, for the most part, to the propositions elucidated by acknowledged writers, statesmen and administrators. This is what has been attempted in the succeeding sections of this chapter.

The Necessity for Government

The necessity and functions of government have been succinctly postulated in the famous Declaration of American Independence adopted on July 4, 1776, by the Continental Congress of American Colonies. These colonies had been struggling since long against domination by Britain but the overt parting of ways with the mother country began in 1763. Twelve years later on 18 April, 1775, the first blood of the war for American independence was shed when eight Americans were killed in an engagement with British troops. Thereafter on 10 May, 1776, the Continental Congress, meeting at Philadelphia finally adopted a resolution to "cut the Gordian Knot". On 7 June, 1776 a resolution was introduced declaring in favour of independence, foreign alliance, and American federation. Immediately a committee was appointed to prepare a formal declaration "setting forth the causes which impelled us to this mighty resolution", and a committee of five headed by Thomas Jefferson was entrusted with drafting the document. The declaration opened with the words:

> "We hold these truths to be self-evident that all men are created equal; that they are endowed by their Creator with certain inalienable rights; that among these are life, liberty and the pursuit of happiness; that to secure these rights, governments are instituted among men, deriving their just powers from the consent of the governed; that whenever any form of government becomes destructive of these ends, it is the right of the people to alter or to abolish it, and to institute a new government, laying its foundation on such principles, and organising its powers in such form, as to them shall seem most likely to effect their safety and happiness."

This declaration not only announced the birth of a new nation, but also set forth a philosophy of human freedom through well-constituted governments which are necessary for the happiness of mankind. The principle underlying the declaration commands support throughout the civilized world.

The "truths" embodied in the declaration were not the creation of Jefferson. They were parts of a political theory "self-evident" to his contemporaries and to most thinkers after him. He was then only 33 years old, but had already established a reputation for learning. No more suitable person could have been chosen to draft the great declaration. Jefferson later became the third President of the United States. The sources of Jefferson's thinking and phraseology are to be found in James Harrington's Oceana and John Locke's Second Treatise on Government—works of English political thinkers. But though the phraseology was derived from theoretical discussions in the works mentioned, the source of the spirit of the document was the awakening consciousness of men that government should exist for the people, not the people for the government. To Jefferson, it was the function and purpose of the government to help men—to protect them in their life, their liberty, and their pursuit of happiness—not to oppress them or misuse them.

Role of Administrator in Policy Formulation[2]

What is policy? The dictionary defines policy as 'a course of action adopted and pursued by a government, party, ruler, State, etc.' It includes 'any course of action adopted as advantageous or expedient'. There are other meanings of the word, namely 'sagacity, shrewdness, artfulness, cunningness, craftiness' but these are inapplicable to the present discussion.

According to Luther Gullick, discretion is the essential element in the determination of policy—"anyone who has discretion determines policy, even the most minor employee." Though an overstatement, this illustrates the wide interpretation that can be given to policy-making.

The above descriptions are, however, not much helpful in conveying the subtle implications of the word 'policy', but it is not necessary to go into an academic analysis since the import of the word is well understood by administrative officers. Policies frequently fan out from some central objective. Thus, the basic objective of India's development programmes is to provide the masses with opportunities to lead a good life. Out of this central purpose come out the policies and services, like financial policy, industrialisation policy, and so on.

Process of Policy Making

This process embraces the machinery of government at the highest level which means:

(a) the elected Parliament (or Legislature);
(b) the government as the majority group in Parliament or Legislature;
(c) the executive government (the Cabinet);
(d) the individual Ministers;
(e) the Secretaries to Government, and
(f) heads of departments and other senior administrative officers.

The Ministers, as members of the Cabinet, have a collective responsibility, and as individuals, an individual Minister's responsibility. The collective responsibility arises from the fact that they are members of a government in whose name (formally in President's or Governor's name, as the case may be) the administration is run. There is also their collective responsibility as Members of Parliament or State Legislature.

Individually, a Minister is responsible for the administration of such departments and statutory authorities as are allocated to him, including the administration of the laws and regulations with which those departments or authorities are concerned.

Matters which are outside the Minister's individual responsibility have to be taken by him to the Council of Ministers agreeably with the Rules of Business.[3] In general new policies and other important matters are so referred. An impelling influence towards collective decision is that a major change of policy normally necessitates a new law or a change in the existing law which must be debated by the whole executive government before being laid before Parliament or the Legislature.

Another circumstance which brings the matter before Parliament is the supply of funds needed for the new policy and the power to grant the supply vest in Parliament.

At various points within the administrative machinery it may become necessary to initiate action for a new or changed policy. For example, it may come from the government in fulfilment of an election promise; it may arise from a public demand. It can also develop from the experience of a department in the day-to-day administration of its functions. Sometimes it can generate from an external source such as the world trends making an impact on defence or trade policy. But whatever may be the reason for the framing of a new policy or the modification of a subsisting policy, it is government as a whole which does the job. And the doing of this job brings into picture the administrative officers to whose role we shall now turn.

The Administrator's Role

There is a general belief that 'Ministers makes policy, public servants administer it.' Technically, this may be so, but fundamentally it is not possible to separate the two—the 'policy' and the 'administration' are integral parts of the same function. For an analysis we may turn to J. Donald Kingsley: "The governmental process involves the performance of three related sorts of functions:

(a) "There is, first of all, the function of collecting the detailed information and formulating the experience upon which successful policy can be made. Its performance is primarily the task of the civil service.

(b) "There is secondly the function of taking decisions upon the basis of available information or the actual formulation of policy. This is primarily the responsibility of the Cabinet and Parliament, but its performance is increasingly shared with the permanent officials.

(c) "Finally there is the function of policy execution. Responsibility for the exercise of this function is principally in the hands of ministers, but is actually carried out by the civil service.

"The civil service thus plays a major role in the performance of each of the basic governmental functions."[4]

The administrator's responsibility for policy matters has long been recognised by the British. The duties of the administrative class are officially recognised in Britain to be primarily those concerned with the formation of policy.[5] In fact, the British Government's Reorganization Committee formed after the First World War stated that the key class in the whole civil service structure was to be the administrative class which was to consist of those concerned with the formation of policy, with the co-ordination and improvement of the departments of the public service. "It is officers of this class who act as the advisers of the ministers and who place at the disposal of their political chiefs all the knowledge and experience of past policies and present administrative techniques of which only a highly skilled professional service can be complete masters."[6] There is then Leonard White saying: "It is now accepted that considerations of policy seep down from the political overhead into the permanent career service, making it an agent for the refinement of policy as well as for its execution."

An important point to note in this connection is that the administrator does not, for the most part, possess power in his own right, but wields it only to the extent that he can persuade. Here the British example is instructive. The British administrator's considerable power arises from his influence, and he has become influential because he has been competent.

How does he Fulfil his Part?

Judgment on the need for change of an existing policy will often rest on the experience of the administrator, in his interpretation of public reaction, in his attention to administrative tidiness and economy. "If this policy is changed", he would say, "to meet such and such situation" or "if this policy is substituted for such and such, the Government and the public would be better served". He could also say that the trend of any particular line of action over the years requires re-shaping in terms of changed out-look and standard. Finally, it is within his province to say that this or that policy has run its course, that it is no longer producing the social results for which it was devised and so it should be abandoned or recast.

These proposals are the basis on which a policy is initiated or varied. They are valued by the ministry because the "civil servant in the higher ranks has not only a long experience, but also has that mysterious tradition of the office wherein is somehow embalmed the wisdom of past generations..... Of course sometimes it is necessary to react violently against a tradition which was formed for a different state of society." A strong minister may thus follow his own line.

Even clear-cut policies cannot be finally adopted without the parallel consideration of how they can and should be implemented, and when. Again, the minister is no expert in the activities of his department or in the detailed techniques of day-to-day administration. Of course he has general ideas of the political philosophy of his party, but often he is not sure of the particular solution of a problem facing him. Here he must rely on the administrator for facts and advice.

Then, in many fields, governments do not have a clearcut policy. They have a general purpose which becomes specific, and is often altered, in the process of being achieved. Here too the administrator comes into the force.

The position of the administrator also assumes importance because of the preoccupation of the minister with the representations of individual electors and pressure groups, leaving him with little time to supervise his department closely. Then he is also busy attending Cabinet meetings, listening to, and replying to, debates in the House, answering questions, and so on. Then there are deputations to be met, ceremonies to be performed and social engagements to be fulfilled. In some cases the issues facing his department are focused upon him by individuals or pressure groups, but by and large it is left to the administrator to advise, initiate and recommend. If he is a strong officer with a policy of his own, he will materially influence what is done or is to be done.

Initiative in policy formation also passes from the politician to the administrator when major changes have been introduced or accepted: also, when government has no major alterations in mind. The administrator then collects data and submits his policy programme in black and white.

No formula exists as to how advice on policy should be assembled and presented. It is a mixture of experience, analysis of facts, precedents, sound common sense and personal instinct. All the elements of this mixture are not generally available within the knowledge and experience of a single officer or department. Group experience and the experience of other authorities and countries must often come into in. To be able to advise soundly, the administrator has to be a man of affairs and one who takes an avid interest in events at home and abroad.

Now and then there is criticism of the political loyalty of the administrator and it is alleged that he thwarts the policies of government. These statements are largely untrue. They are based partly on inadequate knowledge of the inner working of the administrative machinery, sometimes they are motivated by the necessity for finding a scapegoat for a political programme which has proved either unworkable or unpopular. So far as the conflicting ideologies of political parties are concerned the administrator is neutral and is as ready to scrap the policy of the outgoing party as he was keen to put it in operation when the same party was in power.

An analysis of policy formation, however, shows that even though the administrator may be neutral so far as politics are concerned, he does help to shape policy and legislation. His actions and advice are necessarily influenced by his own ideas of justice and fairplay. He also assesses public demand and responses and here he is the target of various pressures. It is to be added that the convention of civil service impartiality does not mean that the administrator should refrain from pressing upon ministers his own conceptions of high policy. Nor does it mean that he should be coldly objective in suggesting alternatives. Not even that he is a mere registrar of facts.

Civil Service Ethics

The ethics of the services is an integral part of the principles of administration and behaviour. This ethics is separate from the statutory rules governing conduct and behaviour of civil servants. It consists of an undefined code of traditional conduct which the civil servants have been following of their own accord, that is without any external sanction or pressure. The propositions involved are numerous, but here it would suffice to deal only with a couple of them, namely:

(a) political loyalty;

(b) initiative;
(c) 'play-safe' mentality.

Political Loyalty

This means loyalty to the members of the political party in power for the time being—ministers, in other words. It is expected that such a loyalty and a high sense of honour should inspire the administrator in the everyday performance of his duties.

There are, however, some handicaps which confront the administrator in this regard. Thus, there is a fear that the work in which he is engaged might be discussed in Parliament or in the courts. This fear is enlarged by the thought that the minister might let him down. Not all administrators are, however, subject to this fear of review because, if it does come, it is usually difficult to prove that the officer has wilfully disobeyed instructions or acted contrary to the 'public interest', a phrase which is too illusory to admit of concrete conception. The traditions of the service, however, enjoin on him the moral responsibility to shed this mentality and act without fear or favour.

There is then the question of control by the political power. But formal control cannot be completely effective, and if an attempt is made to make control more stringent by strictly limiting the power of the administrator, the potency of the government will diminish. But all said, control is necessary because it causes the administrator to develop a high standard of moral responsibility and eliminates those officers who, lacking in morals, oscillate between two unworthy roles. Firstly, there are those who pander to the whims of the minister, avoiding even to point out the adverse consequences of his actions. Secondly, those who arrogate to themselves the power and responsibility which must finally rest with political leadership. Ethical principles condemns officers following either of these courses.

Effect on Initiative

While political controls over the civil services have their virtue, there is an evil side too. They are negative restrictions against abuse which, of course, serve their purpose. At the same time, they have diminished the capacity and the willingness to take the initiative in many officers. The result is that while they are efficient in handling, for instance, large construction projects and dealing with a mass of routine work they are less successful in innovating and planning to meet new economic, social and administrative needs.

A contributing factor is the minuteness of the numerous restrictions cast upon the civil servant. Much energy is spent in satisfying this or that requirement and in making sure that what he does will not irritate the minister or the parliamentarians. This leaves little time for original thinking and action on constructive lines.

This loss of initiative undermines an administrative officer's ethical standard and rightly creates feelings against him in the various quarters. How he should get over this handicap must be left to the individual judgment and sense of public spirit of each officer. No copybook formula exists on this subject.

Playing-safe Mentality

The erosion of initiative leads us to the connected topic stated in the above heading. Playing safe means economic waste or delaying the solution of some pressing social problem. The rewards for safe and hard work, though done unimaginatively, may be slow but there is certainty about them. On the other hand, the promotion of the man with drive might be rapid, but he also runs the risk of making mistakes, in which event he faces unpleasant consequences. Few officers are prepared to run the risk involved in progressive thinking and dynamic action even though they possess competence and energy.

The cure for this malaise lies in the hands of the political executive. Only sympathetic, yet dynamic ministerial leadership will overcome the tendency to inaction which is the real threat to governmental efficiency.

The structure of parliamentary government is based on the idea that the decisions of political leaders would be based on the examination of the problem by the administrator—an examination which must be comprehensive and objective. If such is not forthcoming and the minister is served with something cooked to suit his personal inclination, then the administrator would have failed to provide the assistance which the State expects from him.

No Political Independence

In running a State democratically, considerable power has to be delegated to senior officers both as executive heads as well as experts. But this does not make them independent of the political power not does it constitute them into a steel frame as understood for I.C.S. officers during British regime. When servants become masters there is an end of democracy. Equally disastrous is the result when an independent civil service turns into a body of courtiers dancing to the tune of their masters. The ideal lies in the mean between the two. In other words, the good administrator ought to serve his master, the people, as represented by the ruling party, wisely, loyally and most of all fearlessly.

What is be to done if he Violently Disagrees?

There are limits to everything, so there is a limit of the extent to which a conscientious and able officer will make himself the instrument of a policy with which he disagrees. When such an officer is faced with the formulation or execution of a policy which does violence to his conscience, what he is proposed to do? Will he associate himself with a reformative policy which he firmly believes will create confusion and indiscipline in his department?

The answer is provided by the tradition of the British civil service. In such a case permanent secretaries have sought a transfer to another ministry or even retirement. The point is that the convention of civil service objectivity and neutrality is not an absolute proposition. It can be maintained only when the directing officer is thoroughly committed morally no less than administratively, to the purpose of the policy at issue. If he is not, then he must vacate his post one way or the other.

The be-all Ethical Standard

This is succinctly formulated by Walter Lippman when he states that "public officials owe their primary allegiance not to the opinion of the voters but to the law, to the criteria of their professions, to the integrity of their arts and sciences in which they work, to their own conscientious and responsible convictions of their duty, within the rules and the frame of reference they have sworn to respect".[7]

And finally, there is the civil service tradition according to which a government servant is not to subordinate his duty to his private interests, nor is he to put himself in a position where his duty and his interests conflict. He is also not to make use of his official position to further those interests nor is he supposed to manage his private affairs in such a way as to allow the suspicion to arise that a trust has been abused or confidence betrayed.[8]

Safeguard against Dictatorship

When an elected administration repeatedly fails to deliver the goods and life becomes miserable, people begin to think of a change to dictatorship. In their calamities they forget that in the long run dictatorship is much worse than a voted government, however inefficient it may be. What, then, is the safeguard against democracy so that the people may not soon begin to repent?

In fact, that safeguard lies in the recognition by all interested parties that a civil service—clothed by the constitutional spirit, responsive to parliamentary sovereignty and sensible to the watchful eye of the legislators—is vital to the continuance of good democracy. Such a service is the only effective tool for the wielding of the central power and the only insurance against dictatorship.

Human Element in Administration[9]

Command theory—Command is as necessary for civil administration as it is in military organization. But military activities are focused upon winning battles in which the soldier in the field must submit to direction without a question. He is called upon to kill and, if necessary, to be killed. In public administration, on the other hand, the use of command has a lesser purpose than it has for a regiment of soldiers or the crew of a flying squadron. The civil servant is not faced with death while doing his work and there is no enemy to defeat. Further, the civil servant has the option to resign and go, but the soldier has no such choice—desertion is a grave offence which might even cost his life. An administrative officer has thus to control and direct his subordinates who are not obliged to take orders to the extent expected of a soldier. His men may resign and go at short notice.

Limitations of Command Theory in Civil Government

In addition to the above handicaps, the administrator works under other limitations too. An administrator soon discovers that his subordinates regard themselves as equal. Often a subordinate official expects more respect from those who work under him than he gives to his superiors. The command-receivers in civil administration are not bound by the rigid loyalty which binds a soldier to the army commander.

In these circumstances, the problems for the administrator is to get his subordinates to develop a will to do rather than fear punishment for their refusal to do. A wise administrator will, therefore, do all his supervising through indirect instead of direct command. He will thus have to be creative in his administration. This leads us to the conclusion that an officer to be successful will concern himself with the development of an attitude of cooperation based mutual respect.

The Requisites of Success

The success of a department, which means the success of its Head, thus depends upon the attitude of the Head and his subordinates towards each other. The days are past when failure to comply was unpardonable. Scolding and reprimand have now lost their potency. Their place has been taken by the morale of the employees which alone can bring about good results. The administrative officer cannot, all the time, afford to take disciplinary proceedings against erring officials. Even if he does, the replaced personnel will be no better.

Constructive Approach through Elimination of Fear

Fear has a deteriorating effect on administrative business as it has on all human activities. In the affairs of the State there is the fear of rule-violation and the resulting punishment, fear of the superior whose mood changes due to personal feelings. The superior himself fears his subordinates who do not appreciate the efforts made by him both for himself and his subordinates: his fear of colleagues who are eager to get ahead of him, fear that still more higher authorities do not value his efforts.

The positive approach, therefore, is to replace fear by confidence. This confidence will be generated:

(a) if appreciation or reward is given when due;
(b) if punishment is awarded not upon the whim of a superior but on proved facts about rule-violation or misconduct;
(c) if promotions are made upon merit;
(d) if those passed over are not altogether neglected; and
(e) if personal problems are met with justness and sympathy and not arbitrarily.

Good morale upset by fear can be restored by confidence. To achieve this the superior need not cajole his subordinates such a course is taken as a deceipt and an index of weakness. At the same time he himself should not yield to flattery from his subordinates.

Factors of Constructive Approach

But these negative aspects need not deter us from addressing ourselves to a positive approach. There are of course no set of rules for promoting respect and cooperation. However, the method adopted by skilled administrators provide a working guidance for the exercise of a purposeful approach to relationship between the officer and his subordinates with a view to achieving results. The more significant of these are listed below:

(a) Setting a personal example is the best way of inspiring confidence. He should listen to complaints which provide an opportunity to remove personal fears and to suggest constructive thinking. Many complaints are based upon wrong premises and when that is clarified the complaint disappears.
(b) Encouragement of 'friendliness' in employer-employee relationship pays.

REFERENCES

1. In the Study of Public Administration. Woodrow Wilson was President of the United States during the First World War. He held the office for two terms (1912-1920).
2. In preparing this section use has been made of an address on the subject by the late Sri A.N. Jha, I.C.S. at the Institute of Public

Administration, Lucknow University, on 17.11.1964. He was then Secretary, Union Ministry of Information and Broadcasting. Later he became Lt. Governor of Delhi.

3. Framed under article 77 of the Constitution by the President and under article 166 by the Governor.
4. J.D. Kingsley in Representative Bureaucracy.
5. Lepawsky.
6. E.N. Gladden.
7. Walter Lippman: *The Public Philosophy*.
8. Cmd. 3037 (1928), Report of the British Board of Enquiry (1928).
9. Acknowledgement is due to the magazine.

FIVE

OBSERVANCE OF THE RULE OF LAW

The 'Rule of Law' is a broad-based conception. In a couple of words, it means that it is the 'law' and not any individual or group of individuals, which rules or governs the people. This proposition embodies the supremacy of law, that is to say, the law is above everything and everyone, that nobody is above the law that all things are to be done according to law and not according to the whim of any individual, however high in position.

Meaning

The meaning of the rule of law as defined by the great constitutional jurist Dicey, may now be stated. According to him, the expression means that not only no man is above the law but that every man, whatever be his rank and condition, is subject to the ordinary law of the realm and is subject to the jurisdiction of ordinary tribunals.

This supremacy of law gives security to the individual as against the functionaries of the executive. Since the rule of law is an integral part of every democratic government, this security and protection in their turn become parts of such governments. And this is the reason why democracy draws votaries in its favour in preference to other forms of government.

A lucid enunciation of the principle of the rule of law was given by the Indian Law Commissioners in their report to the Governor-General of India in Council on the draft of the Code which was eventually put in statute book as the Indian Penal Code 1860. The relevant extract from their report runs—"Your Lordship in Council will see that we have not proposed to, except from the operation of this Code, any of the ancient sovereign houses of India residing within the Company's territories. Whether any such exception ought to be made, is a question which without more accurate knowledge than we possess, we could not venture to decide. We only beg permission most respectfully to observe that the public should be taught to regard as a high and enviable distinction, the privilege of being above the law; that the longer such privileges are suffered to last, the more difficult it is to take them away; and we greatly doubt whether any consideration, except that of public faith solemnly pledged, deserves to be weighed against the advantages of equal justice".

The report went on to add: "The peculiar state of public feeling in this country may render it advisable to frame the law of procedure in such a manner that families of high rank may be dispensed, as far as possible, from the necessity of performing acts, which are here regarded, however unreasonably, as humiliating. But though it may be proper to make wide distinction as respects from, there ought, in our opinion, to be as respects substance, no distinctions except those which the Government is bound by express engagements to make. That a man of rank should be examined with particular ceremonies, or in a particular place, may in the present state of Indian society be highly expedient. But that a man of any rank should be allowed to commit crimes with impunity must, in every state of society, be most pernicious."

The Concept

The conception of the rule of law is not necessarily peculiar to a democratic form of government. There have been monarchs who have governed their subjects strictly according to the rule of law both in letter and spirit. The difference, however, lies in the fact that whereas in case of kings, the observance of the rule of law was dependent on their own will and temperament, the operation of the rule is inherent in democracy.

In the words of Chief Justice, Earl Warren of the United States: "The rule of law is not a new concept. There is no mystery about its principles. Throughout the recorded history of mankind, the rule of law has meant the application of right reason and fairness. All people understand it to carry such a connotation. They know, it means rules governing conduct and decision according to what is morally right to ensure liberty, equality and justice in relationship between men and Government. The rule of law has no boundaries and is in its very nature international in character. All nations have made it a profession of faith."[1]

It might interest the reader if an example be given here from ancient India of a justice-loving king Harishchandra, who sacrificed his son at the alter of the rule of law. Manu Neethi Kondachola, the Chola king in south India vindicated the principle of equality before the law against his own son, the crown prince, whose chariot accidentally ran over and killed a calf. The bereaved cow rang the bell of justice at the palace gate to complain of her loss. It is recorded that the King Kondachola, in response to the cry of the cow, ordained that the prince must pay the penalty for the crime and passed the sentence that the prince himself must be crushed under the wheels of a chariot.

We have also the example of the ancient Greek philosopher Socrates who chose to drink hemlock in preference to placing himself above the law by escaping from prison and thus freeing himself from the penalty of death to which he had been sentenced by his country's judges. He recognised the supremacy of the law although he had been unjustly sentenced to die and this he explained to Crito, his wealthy disciple and declined to flee from punishment although the latter had made arrangements for his safe escape. He recognised that if he had violated the law he must willingly pay the penalty for the breach and not run away from it. In other words, he did not contend that he was above the law.

Similarly, the famous French statesman Rousseau, who had defended the right to resist unjust laws, still conceded that no individual in a democracy should have the right to be above the law. In our own time, Mahatma Gandhi, though he disobeyed the laws to resist the continuance of British Rule in India, gracefully accepted the punishment imposed by courts of justice.

Law as King of Kings

There is then the verdict of a Upanishad in these words: "Law is the King of kings, far more rigid and powerful than they. There is nothing higher than law. By its prowess the weak shall be protected against the strong and justice will triumph". The great law-giver Manu has propounded the rule of law in these memorable words: " If the father, teacher, friend, mother, wife, son or domestic priest failed to attend to their own duties, they should not go unpunished by the king."

The development of the rule of law as an international concept is being fostered by the International Commission of Jurists as is apparent from Article 4 of its statute which states: "The Commission is dedicated to the support and advancement of those principles of justice which constitute the basis of the Rule of Law.... The Commission will foster understanding of, and respect for, the Rule of Law and give aid and encouragement to those people to whom the Rule of Law is denied". This point has been mentioned only incidentally since the subject of international rule of law is outside the scope of the present work.

To the extent, therefore, to which a democratic government respects the rule of law, to that extent the government itself is held in esteem and affection by the people. From the basic conception of the rule of law as described above, two distinct ideas follow:

(i) that no man is punishable or can be lawfully made to suffer in body or goods except for a distinct breach of law established in the ordinary legal manner before the ordinary courts of the land. In this sense the rule of law is contrasted with every system of government based on the exercise by persons in authority of wide, arbitrary or discretionary powers of constraint; and

(ii) that no man is above the law, but that every man, whatever be his rank or condition, is subject to the ordinary law of the land and is amenable to the jurisdiction of ordinary tribunals.

Judicial Side of the Rule of Law

In its broader application, the principle of the rule of law means that the machinery of the government, both on the judicial as well as administrative side, works so as to ensure the all persons are accorded equality of treatment in all matters related to their right and privileges. So far as the judicial side of the principle of the rule of law is concerned, the Constitution contains specific guarantee for equality of treatment before the law and the application of legal procedure in all matters relating to property and person, as for instance:

(a) Article 14 which provides that the state shall not deny to any person equality before the law or the equal protection of the laws.
(b) Article 15 which contains a prohibition against discrimination on grounds only of religion, race, caste, sex or place of birth.
(c) Articles 21 and 31 which provide for protection of life, liberty and property.

The Constitution provides remedies against all these and other fundamental rights guaranteed by it. So far as the application of the rule of law to the judicial side is concerned, that is a matter for the judiciary to consider. The Constitution ensures the independence of the judiciary, so that the people can feel secure in the application of the rule of law by the courts without interference from executive authorities.

The Administrative Side

The observance of the rule of the law by administrative authorities is no less obligatory than by judicial officials.The Judges being trained in law and also having a judicial background are less liable to err on this score than administrative officers whose functions are primarily executive and only secondarily judicial.The nature of their primary work accustoms them to think in terms of policy and expediency and so they are naturally apt to miss the requirements of this rule. Therefore, more emphasis on this subject is needed for them than for judicial officers.

Now, on the executive or administrative side, the principle of the rule of law is secured by providing for adherence to prescribed rules and regulations. Thus, for instance,there are elaborate rules respecting the rights of government servants and the procedure for enforcing those rights. All these rules are statutory rules and derive their authority from the Constitution. A breach of any of the rules is remediable by recourse to a court of law. This, however, is the ultimate remedy and is to be seldom invoked, because there are other remedies open in the form of appeals, representations and memorials to the proper authorities. There is also the Public

Service Commission which has been entrusted with the function of safeguarding the legitimate interests of the services and whose duty is to advise on disciplinary cases of government servants in specified classes of cases.

Similarly, there are elaborate rules for the recruitment of candidates to the public services. These rules are designed to secure fair and equal treatment to all aspirants to public offices. There is, for that purpose, an independent authority in the form of the Public Service Commission through which recruitment is made to a large number of public services either by examination or otherwise, merit being the criterion for selections.

There are then also rules which, though not statutory rules, are binding on the execution for dealing with the grievances of the members of public in matters arising out of the conduct of government servants. There are also rules, some of them statutory, for the relief of general distress amongst the members of the public so that, as far as possible, all individuals may receive fair and equal treatment and there may be no favouritism or discrimination.

As already stated, it is the function of the law courts to enforce the principle of the rule of law in matters of substantive law and procedure, or in other words, matters relating to person and property. As for the executive side, it is the duty of the public officers to ensure that their actions are guided by the rule of law and not by personal factors or other extraneous considerations. It is well for one to remember that, as a government servant, one is a sort of custodian for discharging his duties according to the letter and the spirit of the Constitution by which he has taken an oath. It follows, therefore, that he is not to allow his personal prejudices to influence his official action; as a public officer he has to disregard his personal opinion. It is further to be remembered that the Republic of India has been constituted to secure all its citizens.

"*Justice*, social, economic and political;

Liberty of thought, expression, belief, faith and worship;

Equality of status and of opportunity and to promote among them all;

> *Fraternity*, assuring the dignity of the individual and the unity of the Nation."

In its application to administrative decisions, the rule of law connotes, according to the modern juristic trends, the following propositions:

(a) absence of arbitrary power, particularly when it imposes penalties;

(b) where discretionary power is granted, it is essential to define the manner in which it is to be exercised; and

(c) that every person should be bound by the ordinary law, be he a common man or a public officer.

Support to these propositions is lent by the observations of the Supreme Court in S.C. Jai Singhani vs. Union of India:

> "In this context it is important to emphasise", says V.R. Ramaswami, J., speaking for the Court, "that the absence of arbitrary power is the first essential of the rule of law upon which our whole constitutional system is based. In a system governed by the rule of law discretion, when conferred upon executive authorities, must be confined within clearly defined limits. The rule of law from this point of view means that decisions should be made by the application of known principles and rules and, in general, such decisions should be predictable and the citizen should know where he is. If a decision is taken without any principle or without any rule, it is unpredictable and such a decision is the very antithesis of a decision taken in accordance with the rule of law...." "Law has reached its finest moments" stated Doughlas J. in United States vs. Wunderuck, "when it has freed man from the unlimited discretion on some rule .... Where discretion is absolute, man has always suffered". It is in this sense that the rule of law may be said to be the sworn enemy of caprice. "Discretion," as Lord Mansfield stated in classic terms in the case of John Wilkes, "means sound discretion guided by law. It must be governed by rules, not by humour, it must not be arbitrary, vague and fanciful."

State Liable for Violation of Law

In conclusion, it may be added that in December, 1966 the Supreme Court gave a ruling that the State is as much bound as a common man by the penal provisions of law even where a sentence of fine and imprisonment may be imposed under that law. The court sat in a Full Bench of nine Judges of whom eight decided thus, and dismissed an appeal by the West Bengal Government against the Calcutta High Court's judgment convicting the State and imposing a fine of Rs 250/- for the contravention of Section 218 of the Calcutta Municipal Act, 1951.

The facts of the case were that the State of West Bengal was carrying on the trade of a daily market in Calcutta without obtaining a licence as required by Section 218, of Calcutta Municipal Act, 1951 which provides that every person who carries on any trade in Calcutta shall take out a licence on payment of the prescribed fee. For the year 1960-61, the State Government did not take out a licence, but ran the market. For breach of this rule, the Calcutta Corporation filed a criminal complaint against the State Government. The trying Magistrate acquitted the State on the ground that the government was not bound by the provisions of the Act. On appeal, Calcutta High Court reversed this decision and sentenced the State Government to a fine of Rs. 250/- under Section 541 of the Act, holding that the State Government was as much bound to take out a licence as a common man. Again, on appeal, the Supreme Court upheld the High Court's decision. In that connection, the Court explained that the normal rule of interpretation of statute was that a general Act applies to citizens as well as the State unless it exempts the State from its operation either expressly or by necessary implication. The Court observed that such a construction is also "consistent with the philosophy of equality ensharing in our Constitution..... The State can make an Act, if it chooses, providing for exemption from its operation... such an Act, provided it does not infringe the fundamental rights, will give the necessary relief to the State."

Applying the above proposition to the present case, the Supreme Court found that the Act, in question, contained no express or implied provision exempting the State from its purview. Accordingly, the Court affirmed the soundness of the High Court decision by upholding the conviction and dismissing the State Government's appeal.

This decision provides an instructive example in support of the legal position that all governments in India and their officers are as equally subject to the rule of law as any common man.

> *"A wise man of Athens was asked, 'When injustice would be abolished?'*
> *'When those, who are not wronged, feel as indignant, as those, who are', he said."*
>
> ARTHUR MEE

REFERENCE

1. Article on Marshalling the World's Law Resources, vide issue of 'The Leader' dated April 2, 1967 in Magazine Section.

SIX

CONDUCT AND MISCONDUCT

Every person who joins government service, whether permanent or temporary basis, has to abide by the rules and orders framed by the government concerning his conduct and behaviour. This obligation arises from the fact that employment, whether government or private, is a matter of contract. There are various kinds of contracts one of which is contract for service, or contract for employment. A service contract may be expressed or implied and it is not necessary for a formal deed to be executed for entering into government employment. In fact no such deed is ever executed except in certain special cases when a person with special qualifications is appointed on an adhoc basis and for a limited period to carry out a specified assignment. Such an appointment is called 'contract appointment' and the appointee becomes a 'contract officer.' In his case the conditions of service are regulated by the terms of the contract and not by the rules regarding conduct and other matters applicable to the civil services in general unless the terms of the contract make any such rules applicable to him.

Master and Servant

In a contract for service or employment, there comes into play the relationship between master and servant. In case of private service the common law of master and servant is applicable. In case of government service, on the other hand, there are some special features. For instance there are rules for recruitment, rules of conduct and rules about disciplinary action. But there is one common feature which applies equally to private service and government service, and it is that the servant is under the control of the master and is bound to obey the orders of the master or that the servant is under the command of his master regarding the manner in which he should do his work. A servant is a person who voluntarily agrees during the period of his service to obey the lawful orders of another in respect of the work to be done by him. A master is a person who is legally entitled to give such orders and to have them obeyed. The test is the right to control. Again, as laid down by the Bombay High Court in *Janardan Bhawaniji vs. Dy. Commissioner, Amrawati and others*, a person is said to be a servant where by agreement, express or implied, he places himself under the control of another, the master. A person is under the control of another if he is bound to obey the orders of that other one not only as to the work which he shall execute but also as to the details of the work and the manner of its execution.

Distinction between 'Contract for Service' and 'Contract of Service'

Between government and its servants as also between a private employer and his servants, there is what is technically called contract for service or contract for employment. The attributes of such a contract have been explained above. There is then what is called contract of service (which is quite different from contract for service) in which there is no real relationship of master and servant although one person agrees (or contracts) to serve another. Thus a person entering into a contract of service, strictly so regarded, is only intermittently employed, e.g., every time a patient calls a doctor or visits the latter's consulting room, the doctor holds himself ready to attend such patients generally as with consent to the conditions he imposes, including the payment of whatever fees he chooses to charge. In other words, he is an independent contractor (by contractor is meant a person who enters into contract), who only sometimes is brought into the category of a person 'employed' by someone. He is unrestricted in the manner in which he performs the duties which he undertakes and he owes not the duty of obedience to this employer. In like manner, though the employment of an architect or of a solicitor may be more prolonged, neither of them is debarred by the nature of his contract from carrying out his duties in the manner which seems proper to him and in conformity with professional propriety and professional custom. Thus, in the contemplation of law, they are not servants of those who employ them but are as much independent contractors, as are medical practitioners and dentists.

Regulation of Government Servants' Conduct

The conduct of a government servant is regulated in a twofold manner:

(a) by specific rules of conduct and general orders issued on the subject,

(b) by an unwritten code of conduct.

The specific rules are contained in the Conduct Rules issued by various governments for civil servants under their rule-making process. These are, from time to time, supplemented by executive orders of a general nature. In addition to these there are conduct rules and orders on specific subjects, for instance, conduct of civil servants in relation to elections to Parliament and State Legislatures.

Unwritten Code

It may be explained at the outset that by 'unwritten' code is meant that set of general principles of conduct and behaviour which do not find a specific place in the conduct rules and orders, but which nevertheless are universally recognised as axiomatic. In case of the British civil service a reference to this unwritten code has been made in the Report of the Board of Enquiry appointed by the British Government, in 1928, in these words: "His Majesty's civil service, unlike other great professions, is not, and cannot in the nature of things be, an autonomous profession. In common with the Royal Navy, the Army and the Royal Air Force, it must always be subject to the rules and regulations laid down for its guidance by His Majesty's Government. This written code is, in case of the civil services to be found not only in the statutes but also in Orders in Council, Treasury Circulars and other directions which may from time to time be promulgated, but over and above these the civil service, like every other profession, has its unwritten code of ethics and conduct for which the most effective sanction lies in the public opinion of the service itself, and it is upon the maintenance of a sound and healthy public opinion within the service that its value of efficiency chiefly depends."

The same position is applicable in India also. In other words, the Conduct Rules are not exhaustive with the result that in addition to observing those rules, an officer is also to conduct himself in accordance with the general principles of behaviour which are axiomatic in character. This is partially implied in Rule 3 of the All India Services (Conduct) Rules, 1954, which provides that "every member of the service shall at all times maintain absolute integrity and devotion to duty". A clearer implication is contained in Rule 3(2) of the U.P. Government Servants' Conduct Rules, which requires every civil servant to conduct himself not only in accordance with any specific orders of government regulating behaviour and conduct which may be in force but also in accordance with any implied orders. This means that he must also honour the implications of various orders of government taken as a whole. The above rule indirectly refers to the unwritten code of conduct and implies that civil servants must behave like decent citizens not only in their official capacity but also in their private lives.

Meaning of Misconduct

The word 'misconduct' has not been defined in any statute or statutory rule. Its general implication, however, is that it involves the transgression of some established and definite rule of action, where no discretion is left except what necessity may demand; it is a violation of a definite law, a forbidden act. It differs from carelessness. It comprises positive acts and not mere neglect or failure. Misconduct even if it is an offence under the Indian Penal Code is equally a misconduct. It will be observed that here also the emphasis in on the proper performance of duties on the part of the civil servant.

Distinction between Misconduct and Negligence

Some kinds of negligence may amount to misconduct, others may not. In other words, misconduct and negligence are different notions. Misconduct, that is inconsistent conduct, has to be proved and cannot be inferred, while negligence can be inferred.

Disobedience, When Justified?

There can be cases when disobedience of order is not misconduct; as and when the servant apprehends danger to life or violence to his person from the master, the servant may disobey for the preservation of life. But the general rule is obedience, and wilful disobedience is sufficient ground for dismissal. The master is to be the judge of the circumstances under which the servant's services are required subject to the condition that he is to give only lawful commands. When the command is lawful, the servant is not justified in disobeying it. Thus, a master discharged his maid servant without notice on the ground of her absenting herself one night to see her dying mother. It was held that the dismissal was justified on the grounds of disobedience to a lawful order of the master. The maid's moral obligation to see her mother was held to be not sufficient to excuse her legal obligation.

Instances of Misconduct

Amongst instances of misconduct may be mentioned the use of objectionable and improper language against superior officers. This usually happens in representations by aggrieved officials who sometimes make personal attacks and insinuations against their officers. An example of this is provided by the following extracts from a representation made by a divisional accountant against the adverse remarks recorded in his character roll by his Executive Engineer:

"The Executive Engineer was in the habit of blackmailing the staff for the fulfilment of his own interests. This he used to do by taking false statements from the staff, on bargaining, against the persons whom he wanted to harass and blackmail and used to show these false statements to higher authorities to prejudice them too against the persons concerned. He was in possession of hundreds of such false statements against each and every target including Assistant Engineers.

"The criterion for pleasing this Executive Engineer was other than duty and work. He wanted to get things done against conscience and rules with the result that ..... Division became a centre of trouble and headache for the administration and a loss of lakhs of rupees by way of embezzlement up to the time of this

Executive Engineer. On my part, I was very careful about any lapse in matters of accounts in spite of every obstacle placed in my way by the said Executive Engineer and, therefore, nothing wrong in matters of accounts and cash occurred up to my time".

It did not occur to the representationist that the conduct of the Executive Engineer was not under enquiry; that he, the representationist, had not been invited to produce instances of misconduct against the Executive Engineer. The real point of his representation was that the adverse entry was unjustified and this he could establish by facts and figures and arguments on merits. His representation had no place for making these allegations which did not advance his case in the least. On the contrary, they weakened his case in the eyes of the reviewing authority who felt that, except for mud-slinging, the representation had nothing substantial to urge on the merits of his case.

Another instance of misconduct is provided by the following extract from a note written is a Secretariat file by a Superintendent of the Industries Department and addressed to the Secretary of that department.

"It is not for the Industries Department to criticise the advice of the Law Department nonetheless to prove that it is entirely wrong and so that it reflects utter lack of knowledge regarding the provisions of the Constitution of India the supreme law of the land, which should be kept in view before interpreting the wordings of any Central or State Act. It has, however, fallen on my lot not only to do so but to establish that the advice of the law department shows utter lack of common sense....... I proceed to establish that the advice of the Law Department from beginning to end has been absolutely incorrect."

In the above extract the language used is improper and intemperate for which the Superintendent was chargesheeted for misconduct.

The following is a more serious case:

In UP, a Secretary in a department in the Secretariat sent his order to the Superintendent to fetch a certain file which was instantly required by him. The Superintendent declined to give the file to him, whereupon, on account of the urgency of the case, the Secretary himself went to the department to get the file. The

Superintendent then shouted, in presence of his assistants, a volley of imprecations against the visiting officer in a most offensive language. He then uttered the following sentences to him.

"Go and tell your officer that I have not allowed R.K. Verma to go to you and that I have not attended to the files pending with me. I shall see him myself with a deputation of all my assistants and ask him to frame charges against you. I shall see that you are dismissed from service. Either you shall leave the department or I will."

Serious notice of this behaviour was taken and the Superintendent was charge-sheeted for misconduct, gross insubordination and indiscipline.

Misconduct in Private Life

The ratio deductible from the principles of common law relating to master and servant is that in order to enable a master to take disciplinary action against his servant it is not a condition that the misconduct on the part of the servant must arise within the place of employment and not outside his place of employment. The test in each case is whether the servant is conducting himself in a way inconsistent with the faithful discharge of the obligations undertaken by him either expressly or in an implied manner in accepting the service. The inconsistency may arise on account of any act of the servant either in course of employment or outside it, which injures or has the tendency to injure his master's business or interests or reputation. There is no reason why this principle should not apply to public servants. There is however, one very material difference between the two and that must be kept in view. In the case of a private servant it is the master who by his own discretion decides the question of the disciplinary action to be taken against the servant. In the case of a public servant it is not the master but certain officers of the same master who decide the question, but their powers in that respect are regulated by the Act or the rules framed thereunder.

In a similar case Madho Singh, a constable, had misbehaved with his neighbour on the use of a common latrine. It was contended by him in the course of disciplinary proceedings against him that the misbehaviour, if any, being outside his place of employment, disciplinary action could not be taken. In this plea the enquiry officer observed:

"It is true that there is an appreciable distinction between the two capacities of a public officer—one as a member of the public and the other as a police officer. At the same time, these cannot be regarded as watertight compartments. The delinquent's acts as a member of the public do have a bearing on his character as a police officer and being a police officer he should have acted with unfailing patience, courtesy and acted and refrained from losing his temper."

In the writ petition later filed by the constable, the Bombay High Court upheld the reasoning of the enquiry officer by observing as follows:

"In the instant case, as we have already shown, it was expected of the petitioner, being a police officer, to behave with civility and courteousness with a member of the public even in his private life. It has been found that he has very rudely behaved with Sri Desi. There is no doubt that the petitioner has conducted himself in a way inconsistent with the faithful discharge of his service in as much as he acted contrary to the discipline prescribed for a police officer in Clause (11) of Regulation 64. Such a conduct is likely to bring disrepute to the police force. He has, therefore, exposed himself to the disciplinary action."

The Allahabad High Court also propounded the same proposition in case of one *Laxmi Narain* vs. *District Magistrate* by observing that it is not correct to contend that a civil servant is not answerable to government for misconduct, committed in his private life. Assuming the contention to be correct, the result will be that, however reprehensible or abominable a civil servant's conduct in his private life may be, the government will be powerless to dispense with his services unless and until he commits a criminal offence or commits an act which is specifically prohibited by the U.P. Government Servants' Conduct Rules. This would clothe civil servants with an immunity which would place the government in a position worse than that of an ordinary employer. The power of the State to dispense with the services of any civil servant, though hedged with safeguards contained in Article 311 and other provisions of the Constitution, is real. The limitation imposed by

Article 311 does not restrict the power of the State to dispense with the services of any civil servant for conduct which it considers to be unworthy or unbecoming of an official of the State, nor does it fetter the discretion of the State as to the type of conduct it shall consider what sufficiently blameworthy to merit dismissal or removal. The State has been invested with absolute discretion in this respect. It can demand a certain standard of conduct from civil servants not only when performing their official duties, but in their private lives as well.

Effective Safeguard against Misconduct

Good conduct is partly a gift of nature and partly cultivated. It comprises two components:

(a) the positive side, that is the good factors in one's conduct,

(b) the eliminative side, that is the avoidance of misconduct.

Regarding the eliminative side, the most effective way of avoiding misconduct is to adhere to the path of duty. Misconduct will not touch an officer who performs his duty to the best of his ability. In the words of Lord Krishna:

na hi kalyanakrt kascid durgatim tata gacchati

[A person doing good actions remains free from troubles.) .... *Bhagwat Geeta* 6/40]

It will be seen from the discussion on 'misconduct' in section 3 (Meaning of Misconduct) above, that misconduct is related to the performance of duty. The civil servant is accountable to the State for the proper performance of his duties at all times and eventualities. Failure in this respect amounts to misconduct.

Duke of Windsor's Example

Devotion to public duty is one of the finest traits of British Character. History is full of instances on this subject, but here it would suffice to refer to the case of the Duke of Windsor who, as King Edward VIII, succeeded his father in 1936. Prior to becoming a king he had an affair with Mrs. Simpson, an American lady with her husband living, and the love affair continued even after his accession to the throne. The king had planned to marry this lady who accordingly obtained her divorce. But the British Cabinet was opposed to the marriage, and Prime Minister Baldwin told the king that there were only two alternatives, namely giving up the marriage or giving up the crown. The reasons for the opposition were that Mrs. Simpson was a divorcee and also a commoner, that the British people could not accept such a lady to be the Queen of England. Eventually the king renounced the throne and thereafter married Mrs. Simpson. Upon abdication he was given the title, Duke of Windsor. In his parting message be said,

"You all know the reasons which have impelled me to renounce the throne. But I want you to understand that in making up my mind I did not forget the country or the empire which, as Prince of Wales, and lately as King, I have for 25 years tried to serve. But you must believe me when I tell you that I have found it impossible to carry the heavy burden of responsibility and to discharge my duties as King as I would wish to do, without the help and support of the woman I love."

It will thus be seen that the king gave up a throne in the fulfilment of his public duty. He subordinated his personal interests to those of his country. In so doing he demonstrated the truth of the couplet:

"France is famous for beauty,
England is famous for duty".

The importance of this narration lies in the fact that just as the highest duty of a king is to maintain the dignity of his trust, so the highest duty of an officer is to maintain the prestige of the office he occupies and the traditions of the particular service of which he happens to be a member. An administrative officer, mindful of this principle, will never be guilty of misconduct with anyone in public or private life.

"The world turns aside to let any man pass who knows where he is going. The ability to make up your mind inspires self-confidence; it gives you inner power and it commands the respect of your fellow-men."

—D.S. Jordan

Restrictions on Acceptance of Foreign Titles, etc. by Indians

The position in this respect was clarified by the Union Ministry of External Affairs in a note issued by it in 1954. Government servants are also covered by that note. What follows is a summary of it.

The Constitution lays down in Article 18(2) that no citizen of India shall accept any title from any foreign State. There is, however, no penalty prescribed for a person accepting a title from a foreign or Commonwealth country. Government officials can be prevented from accepting such titles by rules. Common men are not bound by any rules and it is not desirable to legislate a law providing for penalties in such matters. It will be sufficient if such titles are not recognised by the government.

Decorations, honours and awards which do not amount to titles stand on a different footing and are not banned by the Constitution. So far as government servants are concerned, such acceptance is regulated by rules. Normally, permission is not given for accepting any foreign or Commonwealth decoration, honour or award.

Briefly, the general policy of the Government of India in the matter of award of titles and decorations has been as given below:

(i) Because titles are banned by the Constitution, no Indian should accept any title from any other country. There need be no penalty attached to such acceptance. If a common man accepts such a title, the government does not recognize it and disapproves of it.

(ii) As regards decorations, honour and awards which do not amount to titles, there is no constitutional bar against their acceptance, but the government would not normally grant permission for such awards, except in rare cases. There would, normally, be no objection to awards by the Vatican or to awards for brave conduct or social service to which no political significance is attached. However, in all cases of awards of decoration or honour, etc., a prior reference should be made to the government.

(iii) As regards Indians living in British colonies and other Commonwealth countries, whose nationality is doubtful, the government would not apply the constitutional bar or other rules strictly but it would be desirable that reference is made to it in such cases.

Clarification by Government of India

On the basis of the experience gained, the Government of India reviewed the position and took certain fresh decisions which are summarised below:

1. So far as military and civil servants are concerned, permission to accept foreign decorations shall be given only in exceptional circumstances.
2. Decision on this score will be taken by the Government of India and the main factor to be considered will be whether refusal of the decoration would adversely affect the friendly relations between the two countries.
3. Prior to the aforesaid review, certain foreign governments had proposed to confer decorations on some of those government servants who had assisted in the arrangements made in connection with the visit to India of dignitaries of those countries, where this does not qualify for an exceptional category where permission is given for the acceptance of a decoration.
4. Similarly, some foreign governments have expressed the desire to confer decorations at the time of departure of those military and other officers who were posted in those countries. Such decorations are given not for any exceptional service but according to local tradition. Those too cannot be said to fall within the exceptional category.
5. The same will also be applicable to the diplomatic personnel accepting foreign decorations from those countries where they are stationed.

In order to prevent an unpleasant situation arising in future the Government of India had instructed the heads of their missions abroad that they may inform the countries concerned in an informal manner that the Government of India does not consider it proper that Indian citizens be decorated by foreign countries. The External Affairs Ministry also simultaneously informed the foreign and Commonwealth Missions in India informally in the same terms.

Foreign Decoration not to be Worn in India by Military or Civil Officers

The Government of India has also decided that those officers who, in exceptional cases have been permitted to receive foreign decorations should not wear them in India.

CONDUCT TOWARDS THE PUBLIC

In dealing with public, the following points should be kept in mind:

(i) You are easily accessible to them.
(ii) While meeting them, show them proper respect.
(iii) You should give a patient hearing to what they have to say.
(iv) You attend to their grievances promptly and help them whenever possible.
(v) You understand the technique of dealing with local influential persons.

While maintaining your independence of views and actions, you should be able to keep the public leaders with you. The public should feel that you are an officer both for the public as well as for your own subordinates and that you have courage enough to take action against your subordinates or the public, whosoever is at fault. Thus, while you have to protect your subordinates from malicious talks by unscrupulous members of the public, you have, at the same time, also to pay attention towards the honest members of the public complaining against your own subordinates.

Accessibility

In the present system of administration, a Police Officer has to be accessible to the public at all times either in his office or at his home. It does not work these days to have fixed hours for interview on fixed days. Normally, members of the public come to you during office hours but it does happen sometimes that they approach you at other hours also. It will add to your popularity, if in spite of the inconvenience caused, you listen to what they have to say. Thus, you will earn the goodwill of the public and your reputation as an officer who is always willing to hear what anyone has to say, will soon be established. Of course, you have to use your judgment at times so that undesirable members of the public do not constantly harass you by their presence. You will be able to find out, after a short stay in the organization as to who these people are, and it should not be difficult for you to give them the cold shoulder, so as to discourage them from taking undue advantage of your accessibility.

Show Proper Respect

No matter how highly placed you are, any member of the public, who comes to you, is entitled to full respect from you. Therefore, both in your language and action, you should show him proper respect. He should be offered a seat and you should talk to him courteously. Even if you are unable to do his work, he will go back happy, because by your courteous behaviour and correct etiquette, you would have created a good impression on him. Some officers go to the extreme extent of trying to flatter every member of the public, especially the leaders, in order to gain cheap popularity. This cheap flattery, in the long run, is not likely to help you in the administration. Actually, you should be officially correct, which means that you are showing proper courtesy to every member of the public without going out of your way to flatter him.

Giving them a Patient Hearing

Everyone coming to you with a grievance has confidence in you, because otherwise he would not have come to you. He will soon be disillusioned if he feels that his confidence in you was not justified because you failed to give him a patient hearing. Therefore, when anyone comes to you with a complaint or grievance, give him a very patient hearing, make him feel that you are fully interested in his case and that whatever lies in your power, you will do to remove his grievance. The man will go back happy and satisfied that he has been able to seek your help in getting his difficulties removed. Many times, because you are very busy or your nerves are on edge on account of some urgent problem that you are thinking of, you may be tempted to dispose of a visitor swiftly and abruptly. This will be a mistake if you do so. You should try to earn the goodwill of your visitor who comes to you with a grievance.

Look into their Grievances Promptly

It is your duty to look promptly into the grievance of every complainant who comes to you. In this way, you will not only be helping the complainant but will also be improving your own administrative performance. Many mistakes committed by your subordinates will come to your notice through these prompt enquiries. Do not, therefore, forget the complaint as soon as he has left but see that a prompt report is put up before you, after an enquiry and then use your own judgment. The fact that you have been quick to look into in personally, will ginger up your administration.Your subordinates will feel that you keep your eyes open and nothing will pass unnoticed by you. The complainant will also have the satisfaction that his labours in visiting you have not gone in vain and that his complaint has been looked into by you. Many times, it happens that although a complaint has been made to you by a visitor, yet in the routine course of work, no proper attention is paid to it. This is likely to create dissatisfaction among the public. Whenever the complaints are made in writing, it is a good practice to acknowledge these complaints with the remarks that the matter is being looked into. Many a time, one hears public criticising officers that a submitted complaint was not acknowledged. This makes the administration unpopular.

Technique of Dealing with Local Influential Persons

Whether you are a Sub-Inspector in charge of a Police Station or a Circle Officer or a District Superintendent, you will have to keep in close contact with all persons who have local influence in your jurisdiction. Such persons are the mouthpiece of the public and the success of your administration will mostly depend on what they think or speak of you. It is, therefore, necessary to give a patient hearing to their views and complaints and to accommodate them, as far as possible. Sometimes, their complaints may not be correct and they can be told so, but, often their complaints are likely to be correct or partially correct and will require necessary action on your part. The sooner, you make these influential persons realise that your main object is clear and efficient administration, and you are out to achieve this object, the earlier you will find that there is little interference in your work on the part of these persons.

You may find some local leaders interfering, who, in order to maintain their local influence, come to you with various requests. Reasonable requests should be acceded to and all complaints should be looked into but any attempt to bully you into doing a thing which you obviously consider wrong or improper, should firmly be resisted. These leaders, when they find you not very amiable to their unreasonable requests, may try to find out your personal weaknesses and may immediately start blackmailing you. You can deal with such leaders properly only when your personal character and conduct are above reproach. If you have weaknesses yourself, you will be in no position to stop the blackmailing and soon you may find yourself in an vicious circle which you may find difficult to get out of honourably.

Therefore, do not ignore public opinion and do not work in isolation. You should not only try to mobilise public opinion but also convince their leaders regarding your efficiency and the honesty of your purpose.

Technique of Dealing with Informers

The prevention and detection of crime is the main function of the police. As soon as an aggrieved person reports the commission of a crime, the police should start making all possible efforts to trace the criminal. If efforts to apprehend the criminal fail, the prestige of the police suffers and the public lose faith and confidence in the police. Sometimes in its efforts to trace a criminal, the police makes contact with people who know such criminals. When any such person is taken into confidence, he is called an informer. The identity of an informer must always be kept strictly secret for the purpose of the safety of the approver as well as for the accomplishment of the task through him. Such informers are not always true and sincere. They can deceive the police and even put the lives of policemen in danger. On the other hand they can assist the criminals in all possible ways. These persons may also try to benefit themselves by extorting money from the public in the name of the police. When the public comes to know of any such mischief, it does not extend cooperation to the police. Therefore, police must be aware of such consequences and the technique of dealing with approvers.

SEVEN

THE IMPORTANCE OF INTEGRITY IN ADMINISTRATION

The connotations of the term 'integrity' have to be considerably widened. There is, for instance, the manner in which orders of the government are carried out. Words suffer from very great limitations and except in very elementary cases, cannot fully express the intention of the person who utters them. It is possible for a man in authority to write his orders in such a way as to make them capable of a variety of interpretations. An officer, who is too lazy to marshal his thoughts properly and pursue them to their logical conclusions will resort to this subterfuge. So will the man who is afraid to think logically and face the conclusions. Those who shirk responsibility will likewise try to use language which they know is liable to be misinterpreted by those who have to execute orders. They can thus throw the blame on others. All this is, for want of integrity. Similar want is displayed by those who confine themselves to the letter of the official communication, knowing fully well that it is capable of a much wider interpretation and is actually meant to convey a more comprehensive meaning than the words seem to carry. No one can be legally punished for carrying out the latter of the law, but those who knowingly ignore its spirit are guilty of moral turpitude and lapse of integrity. It is cowardice to seek protection behind ambiguous language or merely literal interpretation, and onwards, it must be remembered, can never make a success of an administration. It requires courage of the highest order along with a healthy spirit of adventure which is one of the qualities that must be possessed by an administrator.

Intellectual Honesty

There is one another sphere in which integrity, which may in this context be equated with intellectual honesty, is absolutely essential. Success in democracy depends upon the fullest co-operation between the expert with deep and detailed knowledge of his special subject and the statesman with wide and general grasp of the principles of sound administration and intuitive knowledge or the mind of the people. The function of the man with executive authority is to frame policies and take decisions on question of public importance while it is the function of the expert, whether he is a scientist or an officer in the Secretariat, to tender advice. The person in authority has to weigh the advice, to assess its probable results, material and psychological, adjudge its immediate and distant repercussions and then to accept or reject it. No one can share this responsibility with him and he must have the courage to take upon himself the fullest responsibility for his decision, no matter what the result may be. No one can claim the possession of unerring wisdom. The administrator is to be judged by the results of his actions and in the long run, the people will give him credit for his honesty of purpose even though he may have to suffer for his error of judgment. But the responsibility of the man who has to tender advice is no less great. He must not allow himself to be guided by the likes and dislikes or the probable reactions of the executive head. He has to be true to his conscience. A piece of advice known or felt to be wrong and given with a view to attract favour or avoiding displeasures is a moral crime, sometimes an act of treason against the State. It has to be remembered that such an advice may affect the lives and fortunes of millions of men, born and unborn. The temptation to shape one's advice according to the wishes of the person in authority is great indeed. Dictators have been known to give short shrift to those who display the foolhardiness to give unpalatable advice. As a matter of fact, an advice is often sought not with a view to inviting independent opinion or gaining correct objective information but merely to obtain some kind of a moral support for opinions already formed and policies already formulated. He who invites such an advice very often knows it to be false, but falsehood wrapped in pseudo-scientific or religio-ethical terms and buttressed with precedents with not much of a relevance to recommend them, gives satisfaction to the dictatorial soul. Rulers in a democratic set-up are not dictators but they are not immune from this weakness and though they do not possess the power of punishment which the dictator finds so handy, there is no lack of sycophants even in democracy. It is the duty of the men holding positions of authority to see that no one suffers for his opinion and the person who fearlessly gives his honest opinion is respected.

Forms of Integrity

There are some instances in which integrity has to be displayed in administration if it is to be a success. We, in India, have achieved self-government after a long period of foreign rule. Among the greatest injuries which foreign domination causes is the debasement of the national character of the governed. We have to rise to our full national stature and to work with the fullest determination to make integrity in the widest possible sense the warp and woof of our administrative fabric. Then, and then alone, can we be true to our people.

> *The men who create power make an indispensable contribution to nation's greatness. But the men who question power make a contribution just as indispensable—for they determine whether we use power or power uses us.*
>
> —John F. Kennedy

In a radio talk, Dr. Sampurnanand, a former Chief Minister of Uttar Pradesh enunciated the principle of integrity in these words:

> *That those who run the administration, whether as members of the Government or officials serving under it, should be men of integrity.*

These sounds like a truism but a little consideration will show that it is much more. The efficient running of any type of administration, dictatorial, monarchical or republican, demands absolute personal integrity, in the sense of honesty in money matters, from those who run it at any level in the official hierarchy. Anything less than this leads to corruption and loss of confidence and produces more than the efforts of a political agitator, a sense of disaffection towards and contempt for the government. A person who accepts gratification whether in cash or kind for the performance of his official duty or permits his judgment to be swayed by such gratification, is an enemy of the society and the

State and deserves to be ruthlessly weeded out. Integrity consists not merely in the refusal to accept any reward for the performance of one's duty; an essential ingredient of it is the refusal to part with information of secret or confidential nature which has come to one's knowledge in the course of official work. The temptation to reveal information is sometimes very great, but it has even though the consequences to those in whom one is closely interested may be of a very serious nature. Loyalty to one's friends and relatives may, in such cases, amount to disloyalty to society and State. Members of the government in every system of administration, except in a hereditary monarchy, often find themselves in a difficult position. Those who have raised them to power seem to feel that they have a special claim on them. They would like the State's resources to be utilized to serve their personal, party or factional ends at the cost of the general interest of society. Problems of morality and propriety do not trouble them. On the other hand those who constitute the governments—it is immaterial whether the repository of power is a single individual or a group—should, however, realize that they would be false to the best traditions of government and betray the sacred trust if they were to allow any spirit of partisanship to colour their policies and actions. The position of the government is specially difficult in a democracy where members of the ruling party are answerable to the people and have to seek their confidence at fixed intervals. There is no doubt that many democratic leaders in the past have succumbed, but those who have faith in democracy, on the whole, as the best system of government have to justify that faith by showing that governmental integrity can be of as high as a standard under this system as under any other.

It is only men of the highest character and integrity, in the fullest sense of the word, who can make a success of democracy. There is otherwise always the danger of its degenerating into an oligarchy or a giant machine for graft and self-aggrandisement which can only end in a dictatorship or anarchy.

War on Corruption in Civil Service

In Rajasthan, the Bharatiya Janata Party government headed by Bhairon Singh Shekhawat had taken some laudable initiatives in long-term planning in the power sector and the drive against graft and wasteful administrative expenditure during his five years tenure in the office. The Shekhawat government's campaign against corruption and wasteful expenditure had received the utmost attention of the media. A high-level committee headed by the then Health Minister Lalit Kishore Chaturvedi, had suggested that a more judicious use of State vehicle could cut down petrol expenditure by about Rs 30 crore annually. A number of senior IAS officers, including the Chief Secretary voluntarily, gave up S.T.D. facility of their residential telephones.

The war on corruption, concentrated primarily against government officials, had virtually divided the bureaucracy into two factions particularly as it was well known in official circles that the then Chief Minister trusted not more than half a dozen senior IAS officers. Two orders of the former Chief Minister, one in the form of a letter to the Chief Secretary vide which he had been asked to inquire into the stock exchange membership of four senior officers including two IAS officers and another regarding a probe into loan disbursement by RIICO to the wards and family members of civil servants, had already sparked off a debate among officials. The point in question was, whether it was illegal for the family members of civil servants to seek RIIC assistance for private enterprises. The list of government officers in the "RIICO loan" category should, however, came as an eye-opener for many. The list of about 60 such officers, (about ten of them were IAS officers) including the Chief Secretary and a retired senior IAS officer, who was an active member of the BJP, read like who's who in the state officialdom. The skeptics, though, were quick to point out that the dragnet of the State's anti-corruption department, which would be rechristened as special bureau of investigation (SBI) with more powers, had so far left politicians alone.

INTEGRITY IN ADMINISTRATION

That those who run the administration, whether as members of the government or officials serving under it, should be men of integrity, sounds like truism, but a little consideration will show that it is much more. The efficiency of any type of administration—dictatorial, monarchical or republican—demands absolute personal integrity, in the sense of honesty in money matters, from those who run it at any level in the official hierarchy. Anything less than this leads to corruption and loss of confidence and produces, more than the efforts of a political agitator, a sense of disaffection towards, and contempt for the government. A person who accepts gratification whether in cash or kind for the performance of his official duty, or permits his judgment to be swayed by such gratification is an enemy of society and the State, and deserves to be ruthlessly weeded out. Integrity consists not merely in the refusal to accept any reward for the performance of one's duty; an essential ingredient of it is the refusal to part with information of a secret or confidential nature which has come to one's knowledge in the course of official work. The temptation to reveal information is sometimes very great, but it has to be resisted even though the consequences to those in whom one is closely interested may be of a very serious nature. Loyalty to one's friends and relations may, in such cases, amount to disloyalty to society and the State. Members of the government in every system of administration, except a hereditary monarchy, often find themselves in a difficult position. Those who have raised them to power seem to feel that they have a special claim on them they would like the State's resources to be utilized to serve their personal, party or factional ends at the cost of the general interests of the society. Problems of morality and propriety do not trouble them. Those who constitute the government, however—it is immaterial whether the repository of power is a single individual or a group—on the other hand should realize that they would be false to the best traditions of government and betray the sacred trust laid in them if they were to allow any spirit of partisanship to colour their policies or actions. The position of the government is specially difficult in a democracy where members of the ruling party are answerable to the people and have to seek their confidence at fixed intervals. There is no doubt that many leaders in the past have succumbed, but those who have faith in democracy as on the whole the best system of government have to justify that faith by showing that governmental integrity can be of as high a standard under this system as under any other. It is only men of the highest character and integrity in the fullest sense of the word, who can make democracy a success. There is otherwise always the danger of its degenerating in to an oligarchy or a giant machine for graft and self-aggrandisement which can only end in a dictatorship or anarchy.

Compliance with Government Orders

The connotations of the term "integrity" have to be considerably widened. There is, for instance, the manner in which orders of the government are carried out. Words suffer from very great limitations and, except in very elementary cases, cannot fully express the intentions of the person who utters them. It is possible for a man in authority so to write his orders as to make them capable of a variety of interpretations. An officer who is too lazy to marshal his thoughts properly and pursue them to their logical conclusion will resort to this subterfuge. So will the man who is afraid to think logically and face the conclusions. Those who shirk responsibility will likewise try to use language which they know is liable to be misinterpreted by those who have to execute orders. They can thus throw the blame on others. All this is for want of integrity. Similar want of integrity is displayed by those who confine themselves to the letter of the official communication knowing full well that it is capable of a much wider interpretation and is actually meant to convey a more comprehensive meaning than the words seem to carry. No one can be legally punished for carrying out the letter of the law, but those who knowingly ignore its spirit are guilty of moral turpitude and lapse of integrity. It is cowardice to seek protection behind ambiguous language or merely literal interpretation it must be remembered, can never make a success of an administration. It requires courage to express and implement the truth as one knows it, but courage of the highest order along with a healthy spirit of adventure is one of the qualities that must be possessed by the administration.

Intellectual Honesty

There is one other sphere in which integrity, which may in this context be equated with intellectual honesty, is absolutely essential. Success in democracy depends upon the fullest cooperation between the expert with deep and detailed knowledge of his special discipline and the statesman with a wide and general grasp of the principles of sound administration and an intuitive knowledge of the minds of the people. The function of the man in executive authority is to frame policies and take decision on question of public importance while it is the function of the export, whether he is a scientist or an officer in the Secretariat, to tender advice. The person in authority has to weigh the advice, to assess its probable result—material and psychological—and adjudge its immediate and distant repercussions and then to accept or reject it. No one can share this responsibility with him and he must have the courage to take upon himself the fullest responsibility for his decision, no matter what the result may be. No one can claim the possession of unerring wisdom. The administrator is to be judged by the result of his action and in the long run the people will give him credit for his honesty of purpose even though he may have to suffer for his error of judgment. But the responsibility of the man who has to tender advice is no less great. He must not allow himself to be guided by the like and dislike, or the probable reaction of the executive head. He has to be true to his conscience. A piece of advice known or felt to be wrong and given with a view to attracting favour or avoiding displeasure is a moral crime, sometimes an act of treason against the State. It has to be remembered that such an advice may affect the lives and fortunes of millions of men, born and unborn. The temptation to shape one's advice according to the wishes of the person in authority is great indeed. Dictators have been known to give the short shrift to these who display the foolishness to give unpalatable advice. As a matter of fact, an advice is often sought not with a view to inviting independent opinion or gaining correct objective information but merely to obtain some kind of a moral support for opinions already formed and policies already formulated. He who invites such an advice very often it to be false but falsehood wrapped in pseudoscientific or religio-ethical terms and buttressed up with precedents with not much of a relevance to recommend them which gives satisfaction to the dictatorial soul. Rulers in a democratic set-up are not dictators but they are not immune from this weakness and, though they do not possess the power of punishment which the dictator find so handy, there is no lack of sycophants even in democracy. It is the duty of men holding positions of authority in a democracy to produce in those who serve under them, the confidence that no one will suffer for his opinion and the person who fearlessly gives his honest opinion will be respected.

Integrity has to be Visible

These are some of the forms in which integrity has to be displayed in administration if it is to be a success. We, in India, have achieved self-government after a long period of foreign rule. Among the greatest injuries which foreign domination causes is the debasement of the national character of the governed. We have to rise to the full stature of our nationhood and to work with the fullest determination to make integrity in the widest possible sense the texture and warp and woof of our administrative fabric. Then and then alone we can be true to ourselves and to our people.*

RISING CORRUPTION AND FALLING STANDARDS OF MORALITY

A serious handicap from which the Indian administration suffers is the level of social efficiency and honesty. The result is that the bulk of the civil services is manned by persons who are substandard in discipline, orderliness and devotion to duty. Further, the stress on economic status amongst the persons of that class makes it difficult for them to resist the temptation of easy money. In the words of 'The Pioneer', "No administration can have a higher standard of morality or efficiency than the country's general level of social efficiency or honesty. Corruption, it has been said, is the result of inadequate public morality. It has also a certain close relationship with the degree of economic prosperity that a society has attained. That is one reason why the same administrative

* This talk was the first of a series entitled "Administrative Tasks in the Second Plan" broadcast from the Lucknow Station of All India Radio. It was given by the then Chief Minister, Dr Sampurnanand on February 12, 1957.

system produces more corruption in one State than the other. Often, corruption comes from the public's attempt to get results at the speed it wants instead of the speed which is convenient to the official."

Rising Tide of Corruption

It is in these circumstances that a handful of administrators find it almost impossible to check corruption in spite of numerous government directives in this regard.

There is another handicap which was equally effectively pinpointed in an editorial of 'The Pioneer'. That handicap arises from the direct relationship between the level of administrative efficiency and honesty on the one hand and the level of social efficiency and honesty on the other. This has been brought out by the learned editor in these words—"It is pointed out with a great deal of justice that the efficiency of the administration in India cannot properly be compared with the efficiency of the administration in, say, Britain. It would be more to the point to compare the efficiency of the Indian administration with the general level of efficiency in Indian society and see how this ratio compares with the ratio in Britain. If the office workers in Britain are better disciplined and if the corridors of the British Treasury are silent, it is not a special tribute to the British office worker or to the British Treasury. The characteristics which the British Treasury and the British workers exhibit reflects the general British character, its discipline and its silent efficiency. If, on the other hand, the Indian office worker is unpunctual and if there is noisy informality or untidiness in the corridors of Indian Secretariats, these are merely the characteristics distilled from Indian life. The Government under the British regime in India is generally acknowledged as having been more efficient than the present one."

At the same time it is rightly claimed that India has one of the world's better administrators. Its civil servants are better educated than Australia's, more honest than Latin America's, less subject to political influence than in the United States and more acquainted with the ground realities of life than in Britain.

EIGHT

RED-TAPISM

Since the establishment of modern governments the world over, it has been customary to denounce the amorphous body we call 'Administration', exhorted to cut through 'red tape' and economise on personnel and then suggest the appointment of an 'expert committee' to draw up a list of recommendations for investing the bloated bureaucracy with a new look. This is the general feeling amongst the people that bureaucracy is a body of bunglers, lazy-bones that should either be done away with or truncated.

Red Tape

As for red tape, there is a general temptation on the part of outsiders and politicians to decry red tapism. The politicians in their impatience, want their pet schemes to be implemented swiftly by discarding the rules and procedures which they consider as obstacles. Against this facile and dangerous tendency, Dr. Paul Appleby, the American Consultant in Public Administration, who came to India many years ago at the invitation of the Government of India, sounded a note of warning. He said, "All large organizations and all careful and responsible performances require red tape. A distinguished musician or scientist is one who uses and has mastered the hard and confining discipline of music or science which the uniformed might view as red tape but which is the systematic way of arriving at achievements not possible to pursue effectively in any unsystematic way. Government, more than any private organization, must work in ways preventive of whimsicality and irresponsibility in ways accountable and reviewable and in matter large and more complicated of content than those involved in the largest of private organizations. Red tape in Government is, therefore, fundamentally much more a good than an evil."

DISQUALIFIED FROM TAKING A DECISION

In some cases an officer, otherwise competent to take a decision, is precluded from doing so if he is subject to, what in law is, bias. It is in the following circumstances that bias arises or is presumed:

(a) If he has an interest in the subject-matter of the case, be it financial or otherwise;

(b) If on an earlier occasion he has unequivocally expressed himself for or against any party;

(c) If he himself is a witness in the case;

(d) If he has himself decided the original case, then upon being elevated subsequently to a higher position he cannot again deal with it as an appellate or revisory authority.

In Administrative Matters

The position is regulated by:

(a) Rule 4-A(2) of the All-India Services (Conduct) Rules, 1954;

(b) Rule 19 of the U.P. Government Servants' Conduct Rules, 1956;

(c) Standard No. 3 of Standards of Financial Propriety.

Rule 4-A(2) of the first set of rules provides that where any proposal arises for the award of a contract or exercise of patronage in favour of any firm in which a son, daughter or dependent of an All-India Service Officer is employed, the fact shall be declared by the officer to the government and the case shall thereafter be decided by some other officer of equivalent or superior standing.

Rule 19 of the U.P. Government Servants' Conduct Rules provides that an officer shall not take a decision in respect of a relation, whether distant or near, but shall submit the case to his superior officer explaining the reasons and the nature of relationship. If, however, the officer has not the power to pass final orders but only the function of expressing an opinion, in such a case, then, while he shall be free to express an opinion, he shall at the same time, expressly state the pact, as well as the nature, of relationship.

Standard No. 3 of the Standards of Financial Propriety lays down that no authority should exercise its power of sanctioning expenditure and pass an order which will directly or indirectly be to its own advantage.

Directive of Director-General, Posts and Telegraphs Regarding Decision-Making

In May 1957, the Director-General of Posts and Telegraphs issued a significant circular to all heads of circles and administrative officers on the subject of reluctance to make decisions and assume responsibility. The occasion was a case which had been brought to the notice of the Public Accounts Committee in which appropriate and timely action was not taken against a postmaster reported to have been involved in two successive cases of theft of cash, although the Senior Superintendent of Post Offices, following departmental enquiries, considered that the retention of the postmaster in service after these incidents was full of risk to the department. The result was that the indecision gave further opportunity to the postmaster to commit further misappropriation of government money. The Public Accounts Committee took a very serious view of this case. It felt that the case typified reluctance on the part of officers to make decisions and to assume responsibility for such decisions. The Director-General accordingly issued the following circular of instructions which holds good even today for all government departments.

(a) When powers—financial or administrative—are delegated to a subordinate officer, it is the duty of the latter to see that the delegated powers are actually exercised by him. Every officer should, therefore, thoroughly acquaint himself with the powers delegated to him.

(b) The delegated officer should also ensure that there is no occasion to make a reference to higher authorities in cases which are entirely within his competence.

(c) In cases having important implications, the higher officers should, of course, be kept informed of what is happening, but this does not mean that their orders should be awaited.

(d) Cases in which officers, especially senior officers, shirk their responsibility will be viewed seriously.

(e) Officers at all levels should see that decisions are taken as quickly as possible without prevarication or postponement.

(f) Serious notice will be taken of cases which display unwillingness of officers to assume responsibility or to arrive at quick decisions.

Indiscreet Decisions

There are certain decisions which are perfectly regular and valid, yet for one reason or the other they are indiscreet and for that reason alone ought not to have been taken. It is not possible to enunciate any general parameters which go to make a decision indiscreet, but a couple of examples will make the point clearer than any abstract discussion.

A senior Secretary granted an honorarium to his stenographer for certain special and additional items of work which he was required to do in addition to his normal duties. He devoted considerable time and labour in doing the job with excellence and expedition. The award was perfectly valid and regular in as much as—

(a) the amount granted was within the monetary limit up to which the officer could accord sanction without a reference to higher authority;
(b) the amount was on the conservative side; on merits the grantee deserved a much higher sum and the officer could have granted that without exceeding the limit of his power;
(c) the conditions for the grant of honoraria as laid down in the rules were fully satisfied;
(d) budget provision existed to meet the charge;
(e) no rule or standing order on the subject had been contravened.

And yet the decision was indiscreet.

How to Argue with Senior Officers

Sometimes a junior officer feels that an order passed or some action taken by his senior officer is not, in his view, justified and that the decision should have been different. Now, if the junior officer wants to successfully disagree with the senior officer then, as experience tells us he should keep the following points in view:

(a) Do not argue with him when he is under some pressure, for instance because of some urgent problem facing him or because of tension caused by an event directly connected with his responsibility.

(b) Even when you find a proper receptive opportunity do not bluntly express your disagreement or question his discretion, this will alienate him.

(c) Start your discussion with points you can agree on. This creates in him a willingness to accept your disagreement.

(d) Instead of using such phrases as 'you haven't thought of ....', use such neutral phrases as 'there might be a possibility that ....' and 'perhaps it would be useful to find out if ...'

(e) If the senior officer does change his mind upon your submissions, do not emphasize that point to him. For instance do not end the discussion with the rankling phrase, 'I am glad you see things my way.'

(f) As a rule, avoid disagreeing with him on points of little consequence. Unless your argument is of real importance, and the subject-matter involves serious repercussions, leave the thing alone.

(g) In any case, never disagree with him when there are other people around. Wait till you can find him alone.

Reasonable and Practical Sides of a Decision

The order passed should be both,—

(a) reasonable, and

(b) capable of being implemented in actual practice.

REASONABLE AND UNREASONABLE ORDERS

The most common instances of orders which are unreasonable and for that reason are discarded are—

(a) asking for a report by a stated date which is about to expire or has already expired before the receipt of the order by the subordinate officer;

(b) asking for information within a short period than that which would reasonably be taken in collecting it;

(c) ordering of clearance of backlog of work without supplementing the staff when the existing staff is unable even to cope with current work; and

(d) ordering any item of work to be completed within a few days when it is physically impossible to complete it within a month.

The orders such as these would not be complied with, would seem to be an axiomatic truth, nevertheless such orders are in fact issued every now and then. An officer applying his mind to the orders which he is signing will never issue such impractical orders. It is only when things are done in a mechanical or routine way that such errors occur. The frequent issue of unreasonable orders cause a general tendency amongst the recipients to ignore them. Gradually, and then by habit, this tendency also begins to assert itself, unconsciously sometimes, in the non-compliance of reasonable and proper orders. There is the well-known story of the shepherd boy and the wolf.

Statement of Objects and Reasons

We all know that every Bill brought before a legislative body is accompanied by a 'statement of objects and reasons'. This statement contains a recital of the existing position of the matter to which the Bill relates, the reasons why it is necessary to enact the measure and finally the objects which it is intended to secure. The orders of government and of the officers acting under the authority of government acquire a greater effectiveness if they are similarly drafted. By doing so the reader is taken into confidence and that confidence plays a great part in the implementation of the orders.

Be Receptive and Prompt

While we are on the point of confidence, it would be useful to refer to a matter on which government servants have a general grievance. Representations relating to their personal matters, e.g., pay, promotion, disciplinary matters, are every now and then received from government servants. If they are accepted, well and good but if they are rejected, the rejection has the appearance of an arbitrary order if, as generally happens, no indication of the reason underlying the rejection is given in the communication sent to him. He, therefore, feels, and not unreasonably, that his case has not received full consideration and that it has been rejected on untenable grounds. The rise of such a feeling in him causes frustration and to that extent his utility as a government servant is diminished. Such an officer will have little heart to comply with the orders of his officer in the day-to-day administration. And an increasing body of such officials will be a severe menace to the efficiency of the government. Allied with these cases are also the cases in which a government servant's case remains pending for long and occasions are not wanting when he receives no communication at all on the result of his representation.

There is yet another requirement if full implementation of the orders is to be secured. It will not always do merely to state the reasons underlying the order; an indication ought to be given off the ways and means of fulfilling the order in the form of detailed instructions if the subject-matter demands such a treatment. Without such advice on details, the order would be carried out in a different way by a different officer leading to loss of cohesion and uniformity.

Then again the officers who have been required to undertake a job must be provided with the means of doing it; for example, the funds and the machinery needed, unless these have already been placed at their disposal.

Finally and not the least important is the point that the orders should be worded in polite language which would carry the impression that the person from whom the order is emanating, is no more than a collaborator in a common endeavour in which each one has as important a role to play as the other.

Perfect Order

It is when all these conditions are fulfilled that an order could be said to be 'founded on evidence and reason'. It will then be most willingly obeyed and in doing so everyone will feel the inherent dignity of work and the pleasure of cooperative effort, like a team of players in a sports match.

The question about the reasonableness of an order is one on which no formula can be laid down. In the disposal of a case there are many factors each having its own weight and after weighing all these factors an order has to be passed. The interplay of these factors differs from case to case and it will always be a question for the judgment of the individual officer as to what would be the most reasonable order in all the circumstances of the case. There are, however, a few basic principles which can generally kept in view in passing orders:

(a) The order should be passed keeping in view the 'rule of the law'. By this expression is meant, the application of the same consideration in all cases of a similar kind. That would ensure that the persons who have been affected by the orders, would not complain of discriminatory treatment. For instance, it would not, generally speaking, be right to sanction special casual leave to say two or three assistants of an office and to refuse it in ten other similar cases. May be there are some special factors in a few cases in which special leave has been given, but it would not be possible to bring home these special reasons to the ten others who have been deprived of that concession. The ten assistants would then have the grievance that possibly for extraneous reasons their three colleagues have received a favoured treatment. This is only a simple illustration of the 'rule of the law' but it might help in applying the rule in more difficult cases.

(b) In passing an order the dignity and self-respect of the individual affected ought, at all times, to be maintained. For instance, if an erring official is to be warned, the warning should not be couched in unbecoming or harsh language. It is always possible to issue a warning in language which is both polite and courteous and if that is done, the warned official will not entertain any feeling of animosity towards his superior. The result would be just the opposite if even a well-intentioned warning is expressed in language which might be regarded as offensive from the point of view of the dignity of the individual.

(c) The order passed should have regard more for the larger interest of the public service than be related to personal interest of an individual. All government servants are a sort of trustees of the 'State' and therefore, in passing an order the paramount consideration must be the public interest. Provided that the condition of public interest is fulfilled, it may be possible to accommodate, in varying degrees the personal interest of the affected persons. This may be illustrated by an example. Let us say, there is a question whether an office should be transferred from a district headquarter to a tehsil headquarter within the same district. The transfer would, of course, involve the officer-in-charge. Now, at a district headquarter, there are certain amenities and some better facilities for education than are available at a tehsil headquarter. The transfer would, therefore, adversely affect the personal interest of the employees, but it is established that in the interest of the general public the office should be so transferred. In such circumstances the question of transfer should not be shelved merely to accommodate the personal interest of the employees concerned. So, let us say, an order to transfer has been passed. That having been done, it should be possible to accommodate the interests of the personnel of the extent that instead of making the transfer during the middle of the academic year, the transfer is made at the close of that year so that the officials may be able to make arrangements for the further education of their wards. In such a case the interests of the public service have been secured and to a limited extent the interests of the individual officials too.

Compliance with Orders

The question about the compliance with orders has been discussed at various platforms in the restricted sphere of obedience by government servants, be those orders of the government, or a head of a department or an officer-in-charge of district administration. There is also the larger question of the violation of the laws of the land by people in general. That raises more vital issues and must be left for a separate discussion. All that need be stated here is that as between government and government servants, so between the 'State' and the people, reasonableness must be the determining factor for the executing of orders.

NINE

BUREAUCRACY

As a tribe India's powerful and elitist civil servants tremble at the very mention of the word 'change': The great status quo exists; as they are, what they like best is a certain uncluttered routine and a steady stream of files. Perhaps that's why the panic buttons get pressed in the musty corridors of the secretariat each time there is talk of elections and the possibility to form the new government.

It was around this time a few years ago that the fizz in the bureaucracy vanished. Caught in the midst of an uncertain political climate, the impending polls and the prognosis of the pundits startled them. If Bofors had made them sluggish then the rising crescendo of the opposition stopped them in their tracks. How in the world, they wondered, were they going to cope with such diverse forces as the *Tau* and the *Raja*. After all there was a certain technique in dealing with the Lok Dal, the Janata Party, the Jan Morcha and what have you. The joke was that at least in style, if not substance, the service could claim to have adapted to changing times by declaring a value-based administration.

Ninepin

It is not a well-known principle that whenever there is a change of government his officious not surprisingly the palpitations amongst the babus shows no signs of subsiding. Obviously, the uncertain heart rhythm is a reflection of the continuing uncertainty on the political plane. One's blood pressure is bound to be unsteady. This apart, the prime reason for the poor health of the bureaucracy is the manner in which civil servants have been treated every time there is a change of government in spite of the repeated statements that there would be no major reshuffle of civil servants. Well, they fell like nine pins and got shuffled around in a crazy manner. Look at the list—Home, Defence, External Affairs, Commerce, Industries, Personnel, Petroleum, Agriculture, Fertiliser and several others. Every political party says that there would be no vindictiveness. But the fact is that several officers are always summarily relieved and reverted to their state cadres. And, if that is not enough, it may be mentioned that several officials start cooling their heels waiting for their fresh posting orders as soon as a new government comes to power.

At the top of the heap comes the Cabinet Secretary, who is often chosen to supersede scores of officers to promote his stooge friend, philosopher and guide, who is said to have stuck to his mentor through thick and thin. Moreover, surely the Prime Minister has the prerogative to appoint a few officers of his choice:

Value-based Politics

The rub is that the value-based politics had until the other day dictated that the predecessor be condemned for ignoring convention and traditions. He is roundly castigated for promoting Mr X over two dozen officials including the much later he is once more roundly criticised for failing to appoint the next in turn. Mercifully, in Sheshan's case, the good man was not unceremoniously packed off. With a modicum of dignity and grace, he as given an exalted status and shown the road to Yojna Bhawan. It is virtually like 'Kala Pani' for any self-respecting babu, particularly someone like Sheshan who has tasted they heady whiff of power at the top. Sadly such niceties were dispensed with in the case of the Foreign Secretary S.K. Singh. That the Indian Foreign Service Officers' Association did not even blanch, unlike in the case of A.P. Venketashwaran, when they created an embarrassing ruckus, is clearly a reflection of Singh's equation with some of his comrades or the esteem in which they hold him. But was that reason enough to treat him in the manner in which he was finally dealt with.

If Rajiv Gandhi was naive in sacking off his Foreign Secretary at a news conference, his successor exhibited all the guile and savvy he is so rightfully credited with. He simply wore down Singh's stamina with ruthless manipulation and not so inconsiderable help from Inder Kumar Gujral. When the Foreign

Secretary finally quit in disgust, Vinod Pande moved in like greased lightning to announce his friend Muchkund Dubey's elevation to the job. It will not be out of place to mention that stories in the media like S.K. Singh's cold war with Gujral. These were interspersed with profiles of Dubey. Really? And even if these were true was the Foreign Secretary's exit value-based? And if not, why doesn't someone stand up and say so?

On another plane, one of the first task the new stars in the bureaucratic firmament took upon themselves was to review the work of their predecessors with particular regard to their own clan. Though it may sound contradictory, the hard fact is that if civil servants are status quoists, they are great opportunists as well. A change of guard helps some grind the wheels of fortune a shade their way. Complaints galore were made that there was considerable hanky panky in the manner in which Joint Secretaries, Additional Secretaries and Secretaries had been empanelled by the previous government. In a matter of days the whole list was junked and high level review ordered. The tortuous review has since been complete though a portion of the list is still pending for approval. The list was reviewed by Vinod Pande, Shiromani Sharma (the then Home Secretary), V.G. Dandapani (Secretary, Personnel) and B.G. Deshmukh. And, pray, who had vetted originally? J. Kalyanakrishnan (Sharma's predecessor at Home), Manish Bahel (the Tourism Secretary), T.N. Sheshan and B.G. Deshmukh. These are officers whose value-judgement flunked the litmus test of the new regime so logically they should be suspect in their eyes. And yet they have done rather well for themselves. Sheshan was a member of Hegde's team at the Planning Commission, Deshmukh continues at PMO with the Prime Minister reposing full confidence in him and urging him to continue at his post. And Kalyanakrishnan was selected to head the Union Public Service Commission (UPSC) where he selects future civil servants. A man found unfit to promote officers has now been found fit to select them!

For a moment let's move to the states, only the Janata Dal ruled ones—Bihar, Gujarat, Orissa and later Uttar Pradesh. Hamid Khan, the Union Petroleum Secretary, was shown the unprecedented courtesy of being summarily transferred to his home cadre, Gujarat. He was subsequently appointed by Chimanbhai Patel the then Chief Minister as the Chief Secretary of the State. If his sins wouldn't wash in Delhi, how, one wonders, do they in Gandhi Nagar? Or is it another case of the left hand not knowing what the right does? Or is there a different yardstick for the Centre and the States? In Bihar, the Chief Secretary A.U. Sharma got a taste of things to come, at one of his first meetings with the then Chief Minister Laloo Prasad Yadav. Unmindful that there were people around, Laloo lost his flap and reportedly threatened to hang Sharma from the nearest ceiling fan for his administrative lapses. A shell-shocked Sharma is said to have written to the Union Home Secretary about the incident asking that it be brought to the notice of the Prime Minister.

In Uttar Pradesh, too, the man calling the shots was the then Chief Minister Mulayam Singh Yadav. Most surprisingly, Mulayam had kept the petitioners at a distance. He decline to be cowed down by pressure and had ruthlessly rejected recommendations. Transfers and appointments once affected had to be complied with was Mulayam's dictum. On the odd occasion that someone had dallied, the Chief Minister had hinted of a charge-sheet and administrative action. Moreover, at least as far as the major portfolios were concerned, Mulayam had been far from fussy allowing incumbents to continue.

New Nomilies

Soon after taking over, the new government had announced a series of pious administrative measures. One, that no officer would be given an extension and that those on the verge of superannuation would have to go gracefully. Two, that officers who had spent over five years in the capital would have to go back to their states for the 'cooling off'. It's a rule that had been in vogue earlier but M/S Pande & Co. promised to implement it forcefully. Three, that no superannuation bureaucrat or technocrat would be given a government job. The Cabinet Secretary followed it up with a letter to his fellow officers on some of the do's and don'ts of the business. Most of them after a quarter century of government service were not amused. There were conditions attached to entertainment—who to dine or lunch with and who not to (may be Mr. Pande needs to visit some of the better-known Chinese restaurants of the town to identify the nexus). They were also encouraged to make jottings on the file and be fearless in offering their opinion and not worry about the consequences. The letter brought back memories of the 'dear fellow officers' missive from General Sunderji to his ranks on taking over as the army chief. Despite the honourable intentions, the yardsticks have been adhered to more in the breach rather than form. Many high profile officials, including some in the PMO have spent over five years in Delhi. Logically they should be 'cooling off'. But will they?

And that precisely is the point. Why be holier than thou when you have feet of clay? Each politician has his favourite babu, someone he is easy with, trusts and can hope to share secrets with. Human nature dictates that he would like them to be around him when he comes to power. No one can grudge this much. The trouble beings when there is talk of fair mindedness, impartiality and so on and simultaneously one begins an exercise of hop, step and jump.

Things had come to such a pass in the bureaucracy that the Cabinet Secretary, Mr. V.C. Pande, had felt the need to deliver homilies in writing to all Secretaries to the government explaining that 'it has become necessary to reiterate the obvious because some unfortunate patterns of behaviour have become persistent, 'Mr. Pande had listed out various actions of government servants which are 'reprehensible'.

* Undesirable contact with businessmen of whatever nationality.
* Acceptance of lavish and frequent hospitality from businessmen/individuals having official dealings, and hosting of lavish entertainment at public expense.
* Consumption of alcoholic drinks in public places.
* Sexual harassment of women officials.
* Misuse of vehicles, telephones, accommodation and other facilities owned by government or public sector undertakings.
* Planting stories in the press for furthering private interests or to spread misinformation.
* Acceptance of expensive gifts from individual companies, including foreigners and/or distribution of such items to others at public expense.

* Accepting hospitality from foreigners unless essential in the course of official work.
* Retaining government accommodation beyond authorised period in disregard of government directives.
* Frequent socialisation leading to an impression that some individuals' companies have greater access or influence with the government than others.
* Purchase of shares of companies out of quotas reserved for friends and associates of directors of companies.

The poems of Homer show that a person's destiny is many a time determined by his character. Perhaps in management, we can use the principle: 'Character is career'. A man's career is many a time determined by his character or at least what others perceive to be his character. If a person is perceived to be a hard-working man, he is likely to become a victim of Parkinson's Law. If a person is perceived to be a smooth talker or good in public relations, he is likely to rise more easily than the hard-working person who is a victim to Peter Principle.

You will find many of the victims of the Peter Principle are such barking dog owners who are great workaholics. This aspect has been studies by others and part of the reasons for this also is a sense of inadequacy. If a person who is promoted to higher level is not confident of his new responsibilities, he tends to do the same work which he was doing at a lower level. It means that the organization suffers.

Vittal's Law

The psychology behind red tape also explains the behaviour of victims of Vittal's Law. In every organization there are always knowledgeable persons who are very thorough in rules and remove them, you will find there are very few ways an unwilling worker can avoid work. Of course, one should never underestimate the human ingenuity for coming up with new excuses, but at least the impact of Vittal's Law can be mitigated. A third approach is to simplify our procedures and systems in such a way that buck-passing and cross-referencing are reduced to the minimum. Finally, we should, consciously, also, create a situation whereby genuine work is rewarded. If people find that whose work is recognised and rewarded not only in terms of more work but also in terms of pay, perquisites and promotions, perhaps the predilections for not working may be somewhat reduced. Unless we make a conscious and determined effort to counter the vicious impact of Parkinson's Law, we are bound to be permanently stuck in the quagmire of inefficiency.

Police Officers' Plight

Frankly nothing has been mentioned of the manner in which police officers have been treated here or in the states. Needless to say it follows a pattern as dismal as the IAS. In Bihar Laloo Yadav surpassed himself when he announced vigilance enquiries against senior IPS officers through a press note. There are rumblings within the RAW and IB as well on the manner in which some are being treated at the cost of others.

1. Sunday Magazine, The Hindustan Times, June 17, 1990.

HOW TO BE A SUCCESSFUL BUREAUCRAT*

The International Association of Professional Bureaucrats (INATAPROBU) has its headquarters in Washington, D.C. and its Founder-President is Dr. James H. Boren, who has been an educator, oil company president and an official in the State Department. It has 1,700 members spread over 38 countries. In Boren's own words, this is how the Association was born: "On April 2, 1968, after aggressively fighting bureaucracy in all walks of life, I experienced a sudden conversion during a staff meeting in the State Department. It was a flashing recognition of the errors of my ways. It was the discovery that there can be inspiration in dynamic inaction. I had the sudden urge to show my repentance by becoming an international missionary to preserve and strengthen the bureaucratic way of life. Today I am a born-again bureaucrat."

Here is the Bureaucrat's Creed according to Dr. Boren:

"I believe in the principles of dynamic inaction, and, henceforth, when I do nothing, I will do it with style.

---

* Adopted from The Indian Express Magazine, June 3, 1990.

I believe that red tape should be cut—but as long as it is cut lengthwise.

I believe in innovation and creativity but only as long as it is innovation or creativity within established guidelines.

I believe nothing is impossible until it is sent to a committee.

I believe that to enrich my career, to preserve the status quo, and to make the world safe for bureaucracy, I should live in harmony with the Boren guidelines:

When in charge, ponder.
When in trouble, delegate.
When in doubt, mumble.

Fuzzify

Some of the 'Borenwords' taken from the dictionary section of his book Fuzzify may be of use and interest to Indian bureaucrats.

Retroanalysis— The analysis of past events for the purpose of finding a scapegoat.

Retropunt— To kickback or pay a kickback.

Squattle— To survive a crisis by sitting it out.

Hunkerfy— To mentally crouch or to psychologically prepare to spring in whatever direction may be best for one's career. Skilled hunkerfiers can shift into a state of mental neutrality at the drop of a memo or at the first sign of trouble.

Zilchify— To convert something of value into something of no value.

Bladderate— To drag out or prolong a meeting until it must be adjourned to accommodate the needs of the participants. Often used by those in charge of meetings to withhold a vote or decision until the participants will do anything to get out of the room.

Abstract— To destroy an idea, policy, or concept by making it so abstract that no one, including the abstructor, can understand what is being abstructed.

Boren Advisories

A pick of Boren advisories, reproduced below, may provide food for thought to our bureaucrats as they cool their heels waiting to see their boss.

* Loopholes constitute the fabric of law.

* When a bureaucrat makes a mistake and continues to make it, it usually becomes the new policy.
* You won't get lost if you stay in a rut.
* Never threaten anyone who roosts above you on the organizational chart.
* Sharing ignorance may not lead to wisdom, but it spreads responsibility.
* If you want to control the outcome of a meeting, don't preside; write the minutes.
* Stupidity wrapped in the flag will prevail over wisdom wrapped in the law.

Compared in size and excellence of performance, the Indian bureaucracy is far, far ahead of that of any country and certainly that of the United States, the home of INATAPROBU. It is grossly unfair that in spite of the brilliant achievements of our bureaucracy in assiduously promoting red tape, transforming delay into a fine art and inventing new fashions in flattery and pleasing the boss, the fame and achievements of our bureaucrats have not reached the rest of the world. If the Americans invented the zero base budget, we inverted the zero and imported the magic budget technique, several years after the US Government abandoned it.

The new year brought an agreeable surprise for K.P. Joseph. There was a letter from Jim Boren entrusting him with the task of forming an affiliate of INATAPROBU in India. He was made an Official Recruiter for India with authority to recruit 50 members. Business, academic and professional and government bureaucrats (current or retired) are eligible for membership. The objectives of the organization are to use humour and satire to have fun and to bring about some constructive change.

Because our problems connected with the bureaucracy are peculiarly our own, a great deal of study and planning will be necessary before the organization can start functioning usefully. We have first to discover our bureaucracy. There is an immense treasure of true stories about bureaucratic excellence in India, which has to be brought into the open. A senior official once holding himself up as a model for his department told his officers that he has worked so late and so hard all his life that he never saw the sun set in 25 years, like the old British Empire. He was once received with 27 garlands at an airport—all provided free by the Horticultural Department of a State Government.

Our bureaucrats use imagination while making their travel claims. Some of them can appear at two different places simultaneously or travel in opposite directions. Or travel to far-away places merely sitting at home. Our rules will astonish anyone.

The Secretariat Manual of a State Government has rules teaching the staff how to use a telephone. When you hear the telephone ring, lose no time, hurry, pick up the receiver and say "Hello" loudly and clearly. In the rainy weather, cover the telephone. It also contains instructions for the Viceroy's visit to the state. Where else but in India will you find a primary school with 6 teachers, 25 pupils and 32 cleaners to kept it tidy?

More information from readers about incidents of red tape, flattering the boss, harassing the public, superciliousness, bureaucratic prose or any information about bureaucratic excellence will be most welcome. Suggestions on what types of excellence should be recognised and rewarded will be appreciated.

Meanwhile permission has been sought for adoption of a hymn for the meetings of the Indian unit of the Association. It is borrowed from Lord Aberdare, Chairman of Committees of the House of Lords in Britain.

The Bureaucrat's Hymn

"O Thou, who seest all things below,
Grant that Thy servants may go slow,
That they may study to comply
With regulations, till they die.
Teach us, Lord, to rever, Committees more than common sense,
Impress our minds to make no plan,
But pass the baby when we can.
And when the tempter seems to give
Us feelings of initiative,
Or when, alone, we go too far,
Chastise us with a circular.
Amid war and tumult, fire and storms,
Strengthen us, we pray, with forms.

Thus will thy servants ever be a flock of perfect sleep for Thee".

It is our hope to build up the Indian unit in a way that will match the marvellous display of bureaucratic excellence the country has been enjoying for so long. India must have its place in the bureaucratic sun.

THE REQUISITES OF SUCCESS

The success of a department, which means the successful planning by the Head, depends upon the attitude of the Head and his subordinates towards each other. The days are past when failure to comply was unpardonable. Chastisement and reprimand have now lost their potency. Their place has been taken by the morale of the employees which alone can bring about good results. The administrative officer, cannot at all times, afford to take disciplinary proceedings against erring officials. Even if he does, the replaced personnel will be no better. Therefore, what is required is a constructive approach to eliminate fear from the minds of the subordinates.

Constructive Approach through Elimination of Fear

Fear has a deteriorating effect on administrative business as it has on all human activities. In the affairs of the State there is the fear of rule violation and the resulting punishment, and fear of the superior whose mood changes according to his personal emotions. The superior officer himself fears his subordinates who do not appreciate the efforts made by him both for himself and his subordinates: his fear of colleagues who are eager to get ahead of him, fear that still more higher authorities do not appreciate his efforts. The positive approach, therefore, is to replace fear by confidence. This confidence will be generated:

(a) if appreciation/reward is given where due;
(b) if punishment is awarded not upon the whim of a superior but on proved facts of rule-violation or misconduct;
(c) if promotions are made upon merits;
(d) if those passed over are not altogether neglected; and
(e) if personal problems are met with justness and sympathy and not arbitrarily.

Good morale upset by fear can be restored by confidence. To achieve this, the superior need not cajole his subordinates. Such a course is looked upon as deception and an index of weakness. At the same time, he himself should not yield to flattery from his subordinates. Some officers unnecessarily feel flattered by routine exhibition of courtesy by his subordinates. For example, when he enters a room, the subordinates rise in their seats or open a door for him or light his cigarette. These have reference to his chair and not his personal character or competence. An experienced officer, however, does not mistake the form for the content and easily recognises where sincerity lies.

Factors of Constructive Approach

But these negative aspects need not detain us from addressing ourselves to the positive approach. There are of course no set rules for promotion respect and cooperation. However, the lines adopted by skilled administrators provide a workings guide for the exercise of a purposeful approach in relationship between the officer and his subordinates with a view to achieving results. The most significant of these are listed below:

(a) Setting a personal example is the best way of inspiring confidence. He will listen to complaints which provide an opportunity to remove personal fears and to suggest constructive thinking. Many complaints are based upon wrong promises and when that is clarified, the complaint disappears.

(b) Encouragement of 'friendliness' in employer-employee relationship pays. But friendliness should not necessarily be taken to mean social equality. It means a recognition of sincere efforts and a willingness to hear. The subordinate should not feel that the officer is playing tricks upon him or is regarding him with disdain or treating him as a mere slave-like servant. The officer regards him as one of a team engaged in a common endeavour.

(c) Often the administrator will find that he can gain co-operation and ensure full efforts on the part of his subordinates by a discussion impediments and obstacles.

Sometimes ill-will arises out of small problems if left to take care of themselves.

(d) The administrator understands that the objective is better understanding and not :

(i) a disregard for indiscipline;

(ii) a way of giving what everyone wants;

(iii) a way of allowing the employee-leaders to gain control over the establishment; or

(iv) a way of building up personal popularity on the part of the administrator.

The principle of human relations referred to earlier comes to the aid of the officer who works on these lines, as experienced by seasoned administrators. Patience and understanding on a continuous basis are required for the task of changing attitudes; the result once achieved has to be continually kept up.

This extraordinary letter from the seniormost bureaucrat in the country has gone on to say that "while violation of conduct rules in such cases has always been as offence, serious efforts to enforce them may not always have been taken in the past". Urging the Secretaries to "take serious note of violations of this nature and ensure that Government servants follow the prescribed code of conduct both in letter and spirit," Mr. Pande had said "apart from disciplinary action in serious cases, such misconduct on the part of officers would necessarily form an important input in decisions regarding their promotions, placements, empanelment for Central staffing assignments, etc."

The Purpose

The purpose of this two-page letter dated March 15, 1990 is to emphasise that "a sense of service to the people should not only be observed by the government servants, but also seen to be observed." Senior officers have both to set an example by personal conduct and also to ensure that officers working with them do not deviate from the letter and spirit of the conduct rules. In the same vein, Mr. Pande had written: "The substance and style of functioning of civil servants at all levels must reflect the socio-economic realities of the country and the concerns of the government." He expressed his philosophy in this poem:

** The Government does not run by the Cabinet.
The airbus of state flies on autopilot.

The helmsman cannot care less.
The plane flies itself.
Everyone makes moves,
but there is none to orchestrate them.

From the north block window
What I saw for two years,
Others will observe too—
but as helpless to fight the wrong.

All day, they will make cases
to prove nothing improper was done,
what happened was strictly right.
The wages for such skills are high—
jobs for nephews and nieces,
jaunts by cars and planes,
the official good life.

In catching Ambani
You and I were a bit impudent.
Two hundred people died of cholera.
The punishment was the same.
We got transferred.

The bureaucrats are bewildered by the sudden sermon from their boss. What was the immediate provocation for it? Nobody seems to know. They insist that such a letter is unprecedented. While they are unanimous that many civil servants do not conduct themselves as behoves their office, some of them feel that a general letter like this implies that everybody is being tarred with the same brush.

The Bureaucracy must Try to be like Caesar's Wife

In writing to the Secretaries to the Government about 'some unfortunate patterns of behaviour' which have 'become persistent', the cabinet secretary has done no more than his duty as Head of the Service. But will it turn the tide? The general feeling is that the prevailing administrative culture has taken root too deeply to be eradicated by appeals to a dormant moral sense, threat of punishments or even the example of upright officers. Most of these are dismissed as harmless eccentrics who are rather soft in the head.

The cynical view is that the so-called patterns of behaviour are greatly exaggerated, and that in any case, what is there so objectionable about them? They are convenient, flexible and accommodating. Besides, what in heaven's name is the point of making yourself conspicuous when we all have to sink or swim together? So everyone, or nearly everyone, is in the mad rush with the lemmings. If breakdown or even disaster lies ahead, we are all in it together.

No one can fairly say that the new salary scales are unattractive. They are quite adequate for a modest lifestyle. But very few are content with just that. Emma Duncan in her book entitled *Breaking the Curfew* opens with a dinner party in Karachi where an official on a salary of Pakistani Rs. 9,000 lays down two bottles of Scotch whisky on the table at Rs. 1,000 each. In India, we may not go quite so far, but the notorious party in Chandigarh a few years ago which gave rise to an unsavoury scandal apparently far exceeded Pakistani standards of lavishness.

What is possible, with apparent impunity, in one case, sets the pattern. This is precisely what the Cabinet Secretary has written about. However, there is one difference. In Pakistan, flouting religious *fatwas* on drinking and the normal limits of expenditure is quite openly the way of life. Many of us have seen it firsthand. It is perhaps part and parcel of a typical sort of hospitality. It is done without the least suggestion of guilt. We are furtive about these drinks and dance parties, or used to be until a few years ago. The difference here is that it is all done at someone else's expense. A hotel room is booked in one of the five-star hotels, or a garden house in one of the suburbs is thrown open. Young ladies are in attendance. A rip-roaring time is had by all and the next day everything is forgotten, except the obligation in which the chosen official has been trapped.

Enjoyment at Someone Else's Expense

Enjoyment at someone else's expense is one side of it. The other is what you can get out of the opportunities available, purely by the power of the officer itself. As everyone knows there is much persistent angling for the economic ministries. These need not be elaborated upon. Of the services, after the IAS, the most attractive is customs and excise. The reason is obvious. It will take an enormous effort to extricate ourselves from this prevailing administrative culture. Can we possibly manage to do so?

There are three broad ways of tackling what is basically a moral and cultural evil—fear of punishment, recognition of good work through judicious rewards, and persistent social pressure. All these have proved moderately successful at various times and in various places. Allowing for an element of nostalgia, most people who have lived the biblical three score and ten years, recall the pre-war period of British rule. On the whole, corruption was localised in certain low-ranking services. It could not be seriously claimed that everyone else was incorruptible but standards were set and maintained.

In U.P., for example, a British member of the ICS packed off a refrigerator to his next place of posting, 'by mistake' he claimed. The Governor, Sir Malcolm Hailey, compelled him to resign, and he vanished overnight without a trace. In today's environment an unsolicited offer involving several hundred crores of rupees can be accepted in the face of the recommendations of the high-level technical committee for a particular aircraft, without the suggestion of so much as a blush. At least so the allegation in the FIR goes. The case in subjudice, but the daring of the whole thing takes one's breath away, Or does it really? It passed unnoticed for four years, waiting for a change of government.

Underkill

A well-known columnist recently dubbed the present government's attitude to erring officials as a weakness for 'Underkill'. What he did not realise is that precipitate announcements of punitive action betray political immaturity. Cases have to be carefully examined. Almost within a fortnight after his article appeared, reports were lodged in the Bofors case.

The HDW deal followed and later the Airbus fraud. What we are seeing now is a combination of exhortation, high example and punitive action.

This is the right way of going about setting new patterns of behaviour. One can only hope for the good and stability of this country that these measures will at least be partially successful. There is a lot more of the iceberg that still has to be revealed.

The Poet as Bureaucrat

People say he is rude, suspicious, arrogant. I would prefer to be impatient and—like all men who do a job seriously—brusque. It is the greasy lot I am suspicious of. The politician who fawns on you. The bureaucrat who has all the time in the world to be polite. The journalist who tell you what a great guy you are, beware of this media person. Beware of the fat businessman who offers you lunch at the drop of a hat.

A bureaucrat's psalm may be—

Now Dharma remains one's only friend
    As the business of life shrinks,
Desire yields its hold
    And you establish dialogue
With your intellect.

    Leaving behind the Kaurav year
Now comes alive Yudhisthir.
    Enamoured of the angry Karna,
Impressed by the mighty Bhim,
    Arjun's cleverness,
Nakul's charming looks,
    Sahdev's devotion—
This mind was caught in their deceptions.
    Now Yudhisthir is here.
Unflinching in dharma, trusting in intellect.

TEN

RELEVANCE OF THE HUMAN VALUES IN ADMINISTRATION

The text of the speech delivered to the trainees at the Institute of Management in Government, Trivandrum on 15 December, 1983, by Swami Ranganathananda, in-charge Ramakrishna Math in Hyderabad is given below:

"I have great faith that this country will grow, develop and become a great nation when we have politics and administration in a very healthy state. So whenever I am asked to address administrators in various parts of India, I always accept. I address not only Government administrators, Union and State, but also the big institutions like banks whose functioning has so much to contribute to human development in India".

Erosion of Human Values

This is my interest to orient the human mind in India in terms of the development of the people of India, for that is what is meant by freedom—freedom to build up this nation. It must become a passion in the minds of people and particularly in politics and in administration. We are unhappy and as the years roll by, this human value, this human factor has been eroded. Everything else is there, power is there, money is there. But the human factor is getting eroded. Naturally the developmental process becomes arrested and the meaning of freedom becomes absolutely meaningless. After centuries of political subjection, we attained freedom. We have struggled hard to get this freedom. All the political, social, cultural and spiritual leaders during the freedom struggle always emphasized that we need freedom to shape the destiny of all our people. Today we have that opportunity to build up this great nation.

We fought for freedom and achieved our goal in 1947. It was a great occasion. In fact 15 August was an occasion for ecstasy throughout India. I was in Pakistan at that time. There also the same freedom has come, great ecstasy. The greatest misfortune for our nation is that ecstasy was short-lived. Very soon that ecstasy vanished, everybody unto himself, the devil take the hind most—that policy came to invade the minds and hearts of the people in spite of such gigantic problems such as poverty, backwardness, unemployment, illiteracy, negligence of millions of people, etc. This should have kept us alert, active, dynamic for all these decades. We could have achieved tremendous results. But as it is, some results have come. But, by and large, there has been erosion of the most important element in public life, namely, human values. That is why today all over India the one subject we should discuss is how to inject human values in administration, politics, management, in every field of life. We know the condition of our people, how they have been exploited for centuries. In modern period due to our contact with western culture and the challenge of modern western thought, we started considering how to alter this human situation. It is in that context that India threw up gigantic personalities in the nineteenth century beginning from Raja Rammohun Roy, and towards the end of the this century, we had Swami Vivekananda. In every one of them we can see this human motive as the predominant motive. How can we lift up our people? This is the one consideration in all of them. Swamiji's uniqueness was that he knew India at close quarters. He knew the pulse of this nation, the past history, the glory achieved at one time and the low level to which humanity has been thrown in this country. So when he wandered over the length and breadth of India as a Parivrajaka, a wandering monk, living with saints and sinners, Rajas, untouchables, Hindus, Muslims, Christians, during the period 1889-93, what he saw in India was appalling to him—this neglect of man. Our philosophy speaks highly about manwho is a unique product of creation, unparalleled production of evolution, the finest product of evolution. Man can understand the world, evolution, himself and can break down barriers and rise to the highest level. All this is possible to man, but what he actually saw in India is a truncated humanity. Remember the words 'truncated humanity'. Humanity has not been allowed to grow. Every time you raise your head, somebody beats on your head and you become truncated. You fall down. Millions and millions of people in this condition, he saw throughout India. That was a wonderful experience. His heart opened up and in several letters, he inspired the people of India of that time to work for the people, to raise them, to make them manifest their inborn possibilities and in one letter you find this sentence. "Little can you dream of the ages of tyranny, mental, moral and physical, which has, reduced the image of God which is Man, to a mere beast of burden; the emblem of the divine mother which is woman, to a slave to bear children, and life itself a curse". This is the picture he drew of what he saw in India at that time.

Favourable Climate Available for Developing People Today

From that time onwards, a new impulse was given to India. Here is a great opportunity to build up the manhood, the womanhood of this great country. We have today new sources of strength—modern science and technology and a wonderful new political ideology, i.e., democracy. Every human being can be educated to realise his own dignity, his own worth. So many favourable factors have become available to us in this modern period. Earlier none of these was available. From five to ten centuries ago, individual teachers came with full of human passion. When you study the great saints of these periods of Indian history, they were all human beings, their message was humanistic and they also started movements to establish a humane order in India. Among them the most effective was Guru Nanak, full of that human passion, respect for man, how to bring out possibilities hidden within him. He was one of the greatest teachers of humanism—gentle, strong and fearless and full of human motivation—such great teachers came. But the effect could not be pervasive. They were all temporary. Circumstances were unfavourable. But this modern period has a unique meaning in the whole history of India. It is that meaning that Swami Vivekananda brought out for our development. This modern chapter of India's long history has a tremendous possibility of building up the manhood and womanhood of everyone in this country. We have got new ideologies helpful to us, new technologies which can help us in this matter—modern science, technology, democratic and humanistic ideals along with the tremendous humanism in the heart of every religion—Hinduism, Islam, Christianity, Buddhism, Jainism, Sikhism, etc.

Everyone Unto Himself

Today we can take advantage of all this inspiration and treat India as an anthropological laboratory for the development of a seventh of humanity. One-seventh of humanity lives in this continent. Every educated citizen must be sensitive to this human situation and respond to it. That kind of education is what we need today, but we did not get that education. The humanistic ideals never came through education. Some reading of poetry, history and little knowledge came. But, by and large, all that little knowledge that come to us become concentrated in personal advancement and ambition. We neglected man entirely. Everyone unto himself, as I said earlier. Swamiji wrote in that letter a wonderful sentence. "None lives except they who live for others, the rest are more dead than alive." I would like to repeat this sentence again and again all over India. But I see in India today too many dead people. Alive people are very few. Those who are self-centred, they become dead. They do not have the glory of human life and we are increasing their number enormously since independence. Before that we had a wonderful counting of great people, who were full of humanistic passion. As soon as freedom came that whole thing got dried up. We became intensively individualistic and caring for only oneself. So this "unconcern" has possessed us today almost choking us to death.

Concern for Others

Administration during the British period was a very small institution. But after freedom it has become a vast proliferating institution because we wanted a new type of administration. In the British period it was law and order administration. They were not concerned with national development. But when we became free we put into the Constitution, our great idea and ambition to develop this nation so that a new type of administration came after independence. Every personality in this administrative structure must realise this distinction. What was the British period administration? What is the post-Independence administration? One was law and order administration. The other is developmental administration. How to develop this country? How to develop our people? That is why administration proliferated in various directions with all our five-year plans and so many other things. But that was only in number. The quality did not keep pace with the number. Human motivation became eroded little by little. When the Community Development Projects were inaugurated, the Ministers concerned (who is a close friend), the Secretary of the Department at that time, as well as the Swami used to discuss in Ramakrishna Mission, New Delhi, about the Projects. We were all enthusiastic. It was a wonderful thing. But the whole thing fizzled out in no time. It became dead, dull administration. This is the greatest misfortune of people, who after centuries of political subjection got freedom, but didn't know how to use freedom, did not know how to squeeze it to the fullest advantage of the nation. This is something amazing. What had happened to us? We have highly intelligent people in all the fields. Various other qualities are there but one quality is missing—the concern for others. That is lacking throughout the nation.

Post-Independence Ecstasy Shortlived

Whenever freedom comes, people become ecstatic and that ecstasy helps them to create a new culture and civilization. In Bertrand Russel's famous book *The History of Western Philosophy* there is one episode which he has highlighted from Greek history. The ancient Greeks in the 5th century BC were subjected to political harassment and pressure by the powerful Persian Empire. They attacked Greece, destroyed several parts of the country, even ruined a part of Ethane itself. So the Greeks were harassed by the Persians, but eventually after a decade of hard struggle the tiny Athenian State could muster enough strength to defeat the powerful Persian empire, both on land and on sea. This story he relates but what comes later is the most beautiful thing which can keep us thinking in our country. He said that this decade of political pressure and part slavery were galling to the Greek mind which loved freedom and then when freedom came there was such ecstasy of freedom that in the next five decades the Greeks, in a sort of ecstasy created a culture which has inspired the whole of western civilization thereafter; 480 to 430 BC, these five decades of independence and freedom from the Persian yoke created the greatest artists and thinkers. What we call classical Greek culture is the product of those five decades of exuberant freedom which the Greeks experienced at that time. That is called freedom. If free people are subjected to slavery and they throw sway the slavish yoke, that freedom in them finds expression in that ecstasy of activity in all fields of life. Look at India. We had more than five to six centuries of political subjection. When we broke the shackles of slavery and achieved freedom, that ecstasy should have continued for a century creating the greatest cultural development in the nation. It did not happen. Within a few days all that ecstasy vanished. Everybody forgot the nation.

When you think of that midnight on 15 August, 1947, when the Indian flag went up and the Union Jack came down, Prime Minister Nehru gave a wonderful speech about our tryst with destiny in the Constituent Assembly. What a beautiful time it was! Why did people then forget the nation, the people and freedom? The people became selfish and self-centered. Human values became eroded step by step and then when human values were eroded, other evils came into the system. All this corruption and all the evils you find in India today, they all came only because the central principle was removed from the whole politics and administration of the country, namely, the human values. Gandhiji said, "Close your eyes when you are deciding about a national problem and find out the poorest man and consider what good it will do to him. Then you adopt a policy. You will always be right." All that is there on paper. Plan documents we have in plenty, but it is in implementation that these values are nowhere there. We have wonderful people who are good in planning but very poor in implementation not because we have no brains but we do not have that humanistic impulse that will translate the impulses for the good of the nation. This has to be recaptured once again. Then only our objective will be satisfied.

If only Human Values would Inspire Administration

Thirty-seven years we have done something but how much more we would have achieved if only that human motivation was there? Banishing poverty, illiteracy, various types of bondage from which people suffer. 'This is my country, it is my responsibility—that feeling of involvement is so little present. When we get into administration, we become immediately ossified there. Even in education, such a wonderful subject, people become ossified. I was addressing the Central Institute of Education in Delhi in 1949-50—very early period, so in the course of the lecture. I said quoting Vivekananda "five years a man becomes a school master and he becomes a fool". Then a teacher got up and said, "Swamiji is too generous, two years are quite enough". It just becomes humdrum—no further interest at all. If that is so in education, it is much worse in administration. Here the tendency to become ossified is more especially those who are not field-workers. If you are a field-worker you are in touch with a human situation. Some little humanity may come but even that has got erode in our country. Even if it is a district, you say, "I sit quietly in the office, I do not care what goes on. They will go on asking for this and that, I do not know how to respond". This kind of ossification, this kind of dryness of mind has come all over India today. Just think of a state of full human values inspiring administration. What will be the full human values inspiring administration? What will be the situation then? I will tell you one of my experiences. Western countries may have many faults but they have got this human value system. They respect your rights, they are there to respond to you. You need not go on banging at the door all the time. What is due to you, they will give you. This truth was borne in upon me with a tremendous pressure from one experience in Calcutta. I was the Secretary of the Ramakrishna Mission Institute of Culture in Gole Park in Calcutta, a very tremendous international institution. We have an international guest house and an international scholars' house. About 67 rooms are there. People come, even the Finance Commission members used to be guests in the Institute there. One day, the manager who is a Dutch lady but an English citizen came to me with a beaming face. "I have received my first packet of old age pension from London. I myself never asked for it. I did not know anything, but the letter came from England saying 'you have now attained the age of 60. You are eligible for the pension. Here is the first payment to you." What a wonderful experience! She could not believe it. In India it is unbelievable. But there are people there to say "this is your due and I am here to give it to you." What a wonderful experience! My heart asked this question. When will that day come in this country? When administration becomes humanized, that will happen.

"Freedom"—a Mental Attitude

When we were fighting for freedom we used to describe British Administration as 'Wooden Bureaucracy'. Now if you compare that to this, I should say, it is much worse, it is iron, not even wood; impenetrable. It ought to be completely different today because we belong to this country. Very few people have the feeling. "I belong to this country. These are my people. I am here to serve them. I am here to respond to their difficulties." What is the reason for it? That sense of freedom has not come to us in the inside. Outside, it has come—the British left. I am free, but it does not make me automatically free. Freedom is a mental attitude. That has come to the majority of the people of this country—a mental attitude. I am free, I am free. What I do, I do freely. I am not a slave. In one area of life, you can see the truth of this statement. Free people will work according to the demands on them. This is the work which I have to do. Free people will certainly do it. But if I am not free, I will try to edge about it, trying to cheat the particular situation. So we need somebody to supervise. But free people do not need anybody to supervise the work. There is sense of worth, dignity, self-respect in such free people. A Japanese girl working in a house need nobody to supervise her. She has got a sense of self-respect, a dignity— "I am paid, I do my work." We have not developed that attitude in this country. If I am a free person inwardly, a work is given and I will do it to the best of my ability. I will discharge my responsibility. This is my honour, self-respect and dignity. There you have got the real spirit of freedom. If millions and millions of our people realise that quality of freedom then there is no problem here. But it has not come. We are not free inwardly.

Self-discipline is Part of "Inward" Freedom

Centuries of slavery have gone into the blood of people. I often say there is a slave element in our blood—Red Cell, White Cell and Slave Cell. It is still there. We are not free because if you are free, one lesson is, whatever work you do, you do it as your obligation to society. Nobody need stand watching what you are doing. The second quality of freedom is self-discipline. A slave needs external discipline. But a free man has his own discipline. Swami Vivekananda used to admire the British character. See they know how to obey with self-respect, they know how to command without destroying the self-respect of the commanded person. A free man knows how to command. He also knows how to obey. He won't loss his freedom thereby. We have not achieved that quality in India yet. When we start obeying, we convert it into cringing. When we start commanding, we destroy self-respect of the commanded person. That shows we are not free. Throughout India, you will find this inward freedom we are yet to capture.

The Meaning of "Citizen" and the Feudal Heritage

"I am a free citizen of India". I use that wonderful word in English, 'Citizen'. Most of us do not know what 'citizenship' means. What a beautiful concept! Because of centuries of domination we never had this concept in India. In fact in our 5,000 years of history, we are having a unique experience in the modern period. For the first time, we are all free citizens of a free country. Formerly we were not so. We were only *praja*—subjects or children. *Praja* actually means children. King or ruler is just like a father and we are all children. That is the concept we have till now.

Today it is completely changed. We are not children, we are citizens. We are not subjects, but we are citizens. This little distinction means much in human character and human responses to human situations. We have not grasped this in India. "I am a free citizen of India"—what a wonderful concept! In fact, in all my lectures all over, I stress this point. People will have to realise that primarily their status is as citizens of free India and secondarily as a functionary of the government, as this or that, and then India will rise. You are not a functionary, you have got a central beam, that is the citizenship of India. That is your real personality, but called to perform this function that function or any other function. That consciousness of being a citizen and performing a function is far different from a mere functionary. If I am merely a functionary, when I cease to function I become defunct but a citizen is never defunct.

"I am a free citizen of India. On me depends the welfare of this nation. I have no external king or rulers here. We are all sovereign and free in every sense of the term." This is the concept of citizenship. For us it is a new experience. We were all ruled by some king, some prince, some conqueror and finally the British came and we developed a courtier mentality among the upper classes. The same mentality is there with the lower class. That was the experience throughout. I was in Cochin state and I know what an amount of courtier mentality there was, in people everywhere—durbari mentality. Where is that straight-back individual? What is the meaning of freedom? If people in India become suddenly transformed from 'Praja' to 'citizen', it would be a tremendous change. Once we appreciate it, the whole thing changes. Response to human situation becomes immediately spontaneous: "Here is a fellow citizen. I am a citizen. Everybody is free here." But we can see feudal heritage still in every department— "If somebody comes to my office, I treat him with scant respect. Why, I am a slave, he is also a slave to me." If I am free, I will never think so. I will respond to him. When we study police methods in India, this will be clear. Recently in the newspaper, a whole five columns were devoted to the way we handle this subject. The police force treat any person in India as an animal. If you want to arrest a person, just pull him and kick him into the van. Put him there.

I was addressing the Metropolitan Police Seminar in the Indian Institute of Public Administration in Delhi. In England people are free. Even a criminal is also a free citizen of England. They recognize it there. So when the police arrest him in a crime, they say, "Will you please get into this van?" What a wonderful courtesy! Why, because they are free people. Here we kick him into it. Why? Because we have been kicked by someone so we kick others also. This is the attitude in India. Everywhere else you will find this human value proceeding from free citizenship, and the dignity of man being recognized thereby. When that attitude becomes a normal attitude, everything will automatically change and they will become humanized. That is what has been lacking in India.

A "Responsive" Administration

If anybody goes to an office for a job we call him a job seeker and also call him a job hunter. Once you get a job, your whole attitude must change. You are not a job hunter. You are a responsible individual—responsible to the state and nation; so a responsible administration comes from responsible people— "I am here to respond to the cry of distress from the nation." I used to speak in the Central Secretariat on this subject: "How to make administration humanised? Here is a file. The file is about something. What makes the file alive is the man at the file. If he is alive, the file is alive. If he is dead, the file is more dead. What has happened to India is that the man at the file is more dead than the file itself. He has no concern. He will take his own time. If he has to prepare a pension paper how slow he goes! He has no concern. "Nowhere in the world is there this attitude. They always try to do immediately what is due to a person. This responsiveness is tremendous in all parts of the world. It is so little in this great country of ours, the human response. A person has come with a problem. "I am here to solve this problem. But I look to the letter of the law. When an application comes, I find it is not properly worded, I throw it at his face." Nowhere in the world will you find that happening. Here everyday it happens. "I am here to correct the application. I am here to advise you how to write a proper application." This is called administration with a human face, humanistic administration. As you go lower down, first Central Secretariat, then you come further and further down to the Village Panchayat, intense humanity must be present there. We are dealing with people face to face, touching each other as it were. We are human beings there. But when people become wooden, there will be no progress at all. The mind has become ossified. Then one becomes a drag on development administration.

A New Outlook Required

Development of administration needs a new mind, a new type of attitude, that is human values, recognize human values. You are not dealing with a table or a chair, but dealing with a human being. He or she has some problems. You are there to solve them. That chair of authority which you sit on is not a chair of comfort. It is a chair with a heavy responsibility on your head. Rise to the level of the chair. Our mental awareness must rise to that level.

Our people are hungering for development. Government servants are the instruments of administration. These instruments must become more humanized, more concerned with human development. Then something great will happen. Things will march faster and faster. Whatever achievements we have made so far have not been due to steady progress but mostly wobbly movement. Some good has come, but the real progress will come when this human value becomes embeded in every administration so that his work becomes dynamic. Everything becomes dynamic and the tendency to corruption, and evil will become correspondingly less. Take away human value, the corruption and evil must fill administration and public life. Put human value within and to that extent they will be reduced thereby. We have increased evil in society only because we took away the one central inspiring principle, 'the concern for the next individual'. I was at a big dam site a few months ago. We have spent crores and crores of rupees to build the dam with a view to bringing succour to the people—better agriculture, more income for the people. Now all the money that has been spent there, everything can be upset by the people who handle the irrigation channels. If I do not open the channel and let out water to the field, all the money spent on the dam becomes wasted. That man who controls the channels must have a human sense in him and must open the water so that man gets his water and not selfish, inhuman, and one who says, "give me 100 rupees, then I will open this for you". All over India this is going on everyday. What is the trouble then? That man has not become humanized. He is not a free citizen of India. He is a job hunter. He has managed to get a job and he is concerned with nothing else. He does not say, "On me depends the happiness of the person, he is my man, this is my country". If this attitude is not there, all this money will be simply a waste, as we are seeing every day. Crores and crores of rupees are wasted. The fruits of the crores become very much reduced by the time it reaches the people concerned. It is here that human values come in.

How to Humanize Administration

How to humanize the administration? It is an individual development. Today we have introduced many wonderful subjects in our educational system, which are raising the level of human consciousness. Human consciousness can function from different levels. At one level, people are very selfish, petty, mean and quarrelsome. All these centuries our rural life, for example, was devoted to litigation—for everything go to fight and court. We are the most litigious people in the world. We are quarrelling all the time, because no human value is there. Talk across the table, settle the matter—that attitude is not there. The same thing is continuing today, always quarrels only because that slavish, self-center attitude is there. Today that cannot deliver the goods at all. We have to work together with people, work together for the betterment of the people. That is why our consciousness must be raised to a higher level. That is our responsibility. That is the meaning of education. As soon as a child is educated, he or she must become conscious of the nation, its problems, his own contribution to solving these problems—that kind of education has not come to us, education giving us a sense of social responsibility, national responsibility and how to discharge that responsibility. I use the word 'responsibility' now. I used the word 'freedom' earlier. Now combine these two words. Then only a person becomes a responsible citizen. A person who is free from all the responsibilities cannot be called a citizen. He is only asking for his own welfare. "What has government done to me?" immediately comes into the mind straightaway. True citizenship combines freedom with responsibility. It is this that has been lacking. It is this we have to bring back into administration and all other types of management activities in this country.

The Change of Spirit that must Come

Some time ago a young man came to me. He read Swami Vivekananda's "Lectures from Colombo to Almora" where the subject of human development in India is beautifully expounded. He wrote a letter to his mother about what happened on the way. It is an interesting story. He entered a first class compartment. It was full of passengers, mostly Railway officers. They were criticizing the policies and programmes of government as people generally do. This was going on all the time. This boy was reading the book in a corner. After some time an officer came up to this boy and asked him "Boy, what are you reading?" The boy replied, "..I am reading Swami Vivekananda. He deals with the country's problems and how to develop this nation." The officer took the book from the boy and started reading. Soon he became absorbed in the book in a corner. After some time he looked up and found people talking nonsense. He shouted at them: "What are you talking? Nonsense. All sorts of complaints about this and that. Do you know about this country, about our people? Here is what Swamiji has to say", and he started reading some passages from Swami Vivekananda's book. "Mother", writes the boy, "the whole atmosphere in the compartment suddenly changed. All the complaining attitude changed. This is a country, this is a people. They need our touch. We are here for it. Throughout the journey up to Banaras, this was the change. I noticed." Now this is the change that has to come to the whole nation.

When I speak in Secretariats, I often say people talk 'three P's'. They talk Pay, Prospects, Promotion, nothing else. "What to do for the people? What is my responsibility to the nation?" This is not there. P.P.P: only one language is there. So long as that continues, we shall have a wooden administration. Human values would be nowhere there. The country will be grovelling in this kind of suffering, which has been going on for centuries. But in my life time I want to make a change. If that attitude comes, what a wonderful change will come to the nation! We must develop this administration into a suitable instrument for human development in India. The only way to do so is by injecting human values into administration. We are dealing with human beings, the problems of one-seventh of humanity, the greatest opportunity we have in our time. Our grandchildren will have a happy life to live, every citizen will be educated, employment for everybody will be there, clean roads, drinking water supply will be there, what a beautiful picture of India shines before us! But it cannot come by merely shouting or by praying: we have to work hard for it. That hard work is what we need, motivated by human development. This must possess the minds of the people. Anyone who joins the administration must be possessed by this attitude. Then only a real developmental administration will set in this great country. Often people compare what Japan achieved in such a short time. I was there in 1958, when I saw Hiroshima. I lived in Hiroshima addressing the universities there. Such a devastated country. All its shipping gone, harbours gone, everything gone. But in a few years it has built up into a mighty challenging State and today challenging the most powerful state namely America. How did they achieve it? By human values. Remember that. Absolute sense of human values. "Here is Japan, my country, my people, I must work hard to build up Japan"—this is the spirit of the Japanese people. We do not have that spirit. If there is anything that we have, it is how to obstruct progress in the nation. Whether it is labour, whether it is the management, upper level, lower level, that kind of cumulative effort to build up the nation is not there. When I first read about our Iddikki troubles—such a beautiful project; Canadian aided Rs. 30 crores, went on suffering from labour troubles. After some decades the cost went up so much. Why? because this concept was not there, that we are working for our people, for our nation. This thinking is not there in any segment of the population. No wonder we are wobbling, we are not marching towards the goal. That progress towards the goal will come when this attitude becomes the normal attitude of people in the administration. Here is citizenship in the true sense of the term "I am a citizen of India. I have a responsibility to my nation. I am here to discharge it through this particular work or that particular work." Whether you are a doctor, engineer, administrator, whatever be the line of your work, you are essentially a citizen of India and you are discharging your citizenship responsibilities through the particular work you are doing. That work becomes sacred. That work becomes great thereby. I often used to wonder what is happening to education. In Andhra Pradesh where I live, there are so many schoolteachers who take the salary, and never go to school at all. I often used to feel to what a low level the mind has come. Take salary and do not work! It is stealing. But what does it matter? Stealing is normal. I heard in Punjab from a great administrator there—a new method of cheating. A teacher gets Rs. 5000 in the high school. He sub-lets his job for Rs. 1500 to somebody, and enjoys Rs. 3500. A sub-letting, something new. All the evils which other parts of the world do plus many new original evils we have been contriving since we became free. That is why a heaven which was on 15 August 1947, is a hell just now. From the human point of view this is hell. I cannot trust you and vice versa. How can you believe that this is a happy, healthy country? This must go into the soul of the nation like an iron entering the soul. I do not want my nation to be like this. I want my nation to be healthy and strong. To be called a developing nation is an insult to us. 'It is a highly developed nation'; that attitude must come. In near future a little change in attitude and tremendous progress will come in the whole nation. You will catch up with problems step by step. In the next decade we will be able to say that we have established a stage where everybody has the minimum needs for human development. Then we can say good Speed, go ahead. That attitude we must develop today, that intensification of the humanistic impulse in administration so that we can catch up with problems. After some decades we must say India is now a developed country, starvation is not there, decent living is there for all people, education is there, well-being is there, this kind of conviction must come. Today's young people who enter the administration they will say in near future "Yes, our country is quite developed now. I have my contribution to make which I am going to do just now". This is the attitude we have to develop today. Very often we want the other man to do everything. Let him do first. I do not care for myself. That is a very wrong attitude. Swamiji used to tell the story of a king who had a number of *durbaris* (courtiers) of whom he was very proud. His prime minister told him "These are all flatterers, don't trust them". The king said "No, no, they are excellent people, they will never forsake me." The king was very sure. The prime minister maintained that they were absolute flatterers and one could not depend on them. He made a test. He said that the king was going to celebrate a great festival. He wanted every *durbari* to bring a jug of milk and pour it into a cauldron. It was early morning. Darkness was still there. A curtain was drawn. Every *durbari* brought a jug of milk and poured it into the cauldron. The king was now brought by the prime minister to see it. It was only water. The whole cauldron was all water. "What happened?", he asked? The answer was simple. Every *durbari* thought that everybody else would bring milk—"My little jug of water won't be discovered." Everybody thought the same way. So only water went in. We are all *durbaris*, not free citizens, putting fake things, not real things into the administration. When that change will come, we shall say 'yes', we are free, free citizens of a free country.

Our Potential

Imagine about one billion people, all diverse types. How many varieties are there, and we all belong to one nationality, one citizenship. That feeling of fellowship all the time, no caste or creed differences are there. We belong to one tremendous State. What a power we can develop in this country and what an impact a free developed India will have, on the rest of the world and all the impact is going to be beneficial. Nothing bad. India has never acted on the rest of the world in a wrong way. Throughout the ages we have never conquered any nation, though we have military power. That is the blessing of every citizen in India today. The rest of the world is waiting for it. It is not a pious wish, it is serious thinking amongst thinkers in Western countries.

Let me quote only one famous British historian Arnold Toynbee. He was not a devotee of any guru, he was not even religious, he was a historian and critical student. He has written ten volumes: a study of history. He saw something unique in this great country, its past history and its personalities like Ashoka, Ramakrishna and Gandhiji. These are extraordinary manifestations of a soul of people and he writes in the book: "This 20th century had a western beginning, but if the world is to survive it must have an Indian ending." This is a historian's faith. Something wonderful is there in this country. All that is suppressed by our want of human concern. We must express that human concern more and more.

Today India is the largest democracy. We want to cut it to size. We do not want demographic largeness. We want to reduce it still more. But we want to make it the greatest democracy full of great people with sharp minds. This is the type of India we have to keep before us and politics and administration play great part in developing such a nation.

Lessons from Mahabharata

In the Mahabharata you will find a beautiful discussion. Bhishma lying on the 'Sarasayya' addressing Yudhistira on the subject of politics and the ethics of the State. One sentence is there that everything depends upon the political state. If the political state is healthy, everything else is healthy. If that is unhealthy, everything is unhealthy. How true is it today in India! Where many corrupted people are in politics and administration. Today we must realise that truth of Bhishma much more in our society. In fact that portion is famous in the Mahabharata, when all the war was over, for thirty-six years they enjoyed the empire in Delhi. Then the old Gandhari old Yudhishtra with his younger brothers, Vidura and Kunti, said they had enjoyed luxurious life of palaces and were going to the forest forever. They started towards the forest. There was an outcry in the capital at these old people leaving the palace and going to the forest. They persuaded them to stay and not go. But they were adamant. They said let us go and have a quiet life. They were going out of the capital of India, imaging 4000 to 5000 yeas ago. Just going out. Kunti was standing there outside the gate. The Pandavas came one by one, to salute her, to take her blessing. When it came finally to the eldest son, i.e., Yudhistira, the Emperor of India, she blessed him and gave one message. I wish that message enters the heart of all in India today. Looking at this emperor of India, he said:

Nivarthaswa Kurusreshta, Bhimasenadibhissaha,
Dharme Te Dheeyatam Budhih, Manaste Mahadastu Cha

Oh! Yudhistira, go back to the place, continue to rule the State, Nivarthaswa Kurusreshta along with your brothers, Bhimasenadibhissaha, but if you want to rule the State you must develop a new attitude, *Dharmete Dheeyatam Budhi*, let your intellect be established in righteousness, justice, not any particular creed or religion, what is good for the people, what is just, what is righteous and lastly *Manaste Mahadastu Cha*, let your heart be big. A little heart cannot run a great State.

Our Responsibility as Free Citizens

In English we say great events and movements and little minds will go together. If the movement is big, your mind must be big to run that movement. India is a great country. We need great minds with broad attitudes, respect for every religion, respect for every citizen. He may be the poorest humble tribal person, doesn't matter, he is my fellow-citizen, this kind of a big mind, the whole nation must develop today. Then we shall have real progress. We are going backwards, that feeling is there now, but a real feeling will come that we are catching up with problems. We are steadily progressing. That feeling will come with this change in mental attitude and the level of consciousness rising a little higher in millions of people. That miracle we shall achieve in this modern period. This is our responsibility today as free citizens. Nobody else—no Russian, no Chinese, no American—is going to save our nation. We have to save ourselves. This is our responsibility. Whether you are sitting in a metropolitan city or in a tiny village, this is how we can change the whole situation. The subject is of much importance to all of us in India, human values in administration, human values in management and must say I found this human values pervading aspects of life in almost all foreign countries. 'What can I do for you?' It is a constant attitude. If I go late to catch my plane in America, a girl is sitting at the table, she will respond to me, "Swami, you are rather late, the plane is about to leave. Come on. I will quickly take you." She checks up quickly, takes me there and puts me on the plane. We cannot expect that in India. "You have come late, now stew in your own juice." That is the remark you will get here. When will that change come?, "I am here to help you. You are in trouble." When I am in trouble, I want your help. Otherwise I do not need your help. You can help me. This attitude is the human attitude. I hope that state will come, I am feeling hopeful because people want to know, is there a better? This I see all over India, in all departments and among students also, they want to know: is there a better? That is a sign of health.

CONDUCT TOWARDS YOUR SUPERIOR AND BROTHER OFFICERS

In a disciplined organisation it is necessary to work as a team and that is possible only when you are fully loyal and faithful to your senior officers and when your subordinates are in the same way loyal and faithful to you. Therefore, never do a thing at the back of your senior officer, try to by-pass him or keep him in ignorance. Reputation of yourself, your senior officer and the force depend on the loyalty to the force. If you are loyal to your senior officer, you will find that the force will be loyal to you and any deviation on your part will automatically result in corresponding disloyalty on the part of your subordinates to you. Therefore, set an example of yourself so that others may copy and follow you.

Give Your Best

It is necessary for every officer to give his best to his senior officer under whom he may be serving at that time. It is worthwhile remembering that your happiness and success, to a great extent, depend on your relations with your senior officer. You must:

(a) be loyal and faithful to him;
(b) carry out his orders to the best of your ability and in the spirit in which these are required to be carried out;
(c) directly approach him for any difficulties that you may have regarding your work;
(d) go and discuss any problems in which you may have your difference of opinion with him;
(e) bring to his notice any matters of importance regarding the work and discipline of your subordinates;
(f) show him proper respect on all occasions that is due to him; and
(g) frankly apologise for any omissions or mistakes that you may have committed honestly.

Compliance with Orders

The senior officers depend on you for the efficiency of the force. Any orders issued must be complied with fully and promptly. No attempt should be made to comply with the orders in a slip-shod or half-hearted manner. Study the orders carefully and see that these are carried out in the same way as you would like your orders to be obeyed and carried out by your subordinates. This may mean hard work, but this will be worth the labour and the resultant efficiency. Your reports to your senior officer, in compliance with the orders issued, should be completed including the minutes details. These reports will be considered poor, if orders have to be issued to make further enquiries in certain matters which you have failed to include, or enquire into in the original reports.

Contact with Senior Officers

If you have any difficulty in your work, you should not hesitate to go and seek the advice of your senior officer. By virtue of his experience, your senior officer will be able to help you in the right direction. Very often, an officer hesitates to go to his senior thinking that the senior officer will form a poor opinion of him, in case he goes to him for advice. This is a wrong notion and senior officers will always be glad to help you in your difficulties. If a problem is complicated, it is always worthwhile to discuss with your senior officer before dealing with the problem. This, however, should not be taken to mean that for every work entrusted to you, you must go and bother your senior officer. It is only when your difficulties are genuine, that you should approach your senior officer for guidance; but make a rule before approaching a senior officer, you yourself thoroughly understand the problem and that, when you go for discussion with your senior officer, you are fully acquainted with the background of the problem.

Difference of Opinion with the Senior Officer

Sometimes, it happens that you may hold a different opinion than the one expressed by your senior officer. There is nothing wrong in this and before taking further action, it is your duty to go to your senior officer and express your views.

It is quite possible that your senior officer may change his views after having a discussion with you. Sometimes, it so happens that all the facts a senior officer is not aware of. He may modify his views if the extra facts brought to his notice through you, warrant such action. But even after you have had a discussion with your senior officer if his views are unchanged, it is your duty to carry out his orders. No personal consideration regarding difference of views should be allowed to affect your work and you must carry out the orders of your senior officer faithfully and loyally. Do not express either in public or to your subordinates that you hold a different view, that your senior officer had passed a wrong order and that you are forced to comply with it. After you have had a discussion with the senior officer, carry out his order as if they are your own views.

Keep your Senior Officer Fully Informed

It is your duty to bring to the notice of your senior officer all matters of administrative and disciplinary importance relating to your circle and the men under your control. Your senior officer depends on you for being kept posted with all the information and if you are slack and do not pass on the information immediately to him, he may get the information from some other source, which may neither he complete nor authentic. He is not likely to consider you an efficient officer if you are not the first to communicate to him the information. Therefore, always pass on to him all information regarding important administrative and disciplinary details. You have to discriminate and assess yourself what information is of importance and what information is of a routine nature. Every important information should be passed on to the senior officer immediately and routine information can reach him in the routine course. Do not give an opportunity to him to seek information from sources other than you. If you are efficient, alert and keen, you should be the first to get all information about your own group of officers and the men under you and there should be no difficulty in keeping the senior officer well posted with the latest developments.

Respect your Senior Officer

Show proper respect to your senior officer on all occasions. This attitude of yours will, in return, get reciprocal respect for you from your officer. By respect it is not meant that you should be utterly submissive but what is meant, is the respect that you always show to the elders of your family in your talk and behaviour towards them. Be prompt in your salute and in returning the salutes.

Admission of your Mistake

It does sometimes happen that mistakes are made but an honest officer realises them later on. If by chance, you make any mistake or commissions, do not hesitate to admit them and straightaway express your regret to your senior officer. This attitude of yours will be appreciated by your senior officer who will treat your mistakes or omissions with understanding, as he will be convinced that these were not deliberate. If, on the other hand, you wait for your senior officer to find out the mistakes or omissions on your part, you will be putting yourself in a most awkward position, because the officer will ask for your explanation and will be at liberty to form his opinion, which may not be very good for you. He will consider you either inefficient or careless or incapable of forming sound judgement, because you yourself have not been able to detect your mistakes or omissions in time and have made no effort to set them right.

Gain Confidence

In order to be an efficient and successful officer, you must gain the confidence of your senior officer. This you can do only by following carefully the general principles of conduct that have been indicated above. It is very easy to lose the confidence of your senior officer, if he notices even on one or two occasions, that you are not sincere, honest, straightforward and loyal to him; he will drop you like a hot potato.

Conduct towards your Brother Officers

In every district, where you may be posted, you will have to work with your brother officers and officers of the other departments, who have the same rank and status as yourself. It is necessary for you, as an officer, not only to keep in touch with all those brother officers in the district but also to cultivate such personal relationship with them which may enable you to enlist their cooperation in the discharge of your duties. You will find that you will be able to get any particular work done more quickly by talking to your brother officers than having prolonged correspondence. But if your relations with them are not cordial or you have not established any personal contact with them, you will hesitate to discuss with them and will prefer to drag on matters by lengthy correspondence of files.

In order to get help from your brother officers, it is equally necessary for you to give them help whenever they require. If you are accommodating and if you promptly help others in the discharge of their duties, you, in turn, will get their help when you need it. An executive officer, in course of his duties, has to seek co-operation and help of all the brother officers in other departments. Therefore, do not live and move in a narrow group but widen your contacts and know all the officers in the district. For officers of other departments, it may not be very necessary to know you, but you, as an executive officer, have got to know them. Therefore, maintain friendly relations with all of them.

It is not a good policy to speak ill of your brother officers before your subordinates or their subordinates. You will lose the goodwill and friendship of your brother officers by talking of them loosely. Therefore, do not be a party to any loose gossip about any brother officer in the district. It is not proper to speak ill or belittle your brother officer before a superior officer. The intrinsic worth of each officer is generally known to the superior officer and your unkind remarks about him, even if these are correct, are not likely to enhance your image in the eyes of your superior officers. If you are asked a question point-blank by your superior officer about any of your brother officers, you can express your opinion, but only when you are sure. Vague opinions, derogatory to other brother officers, with the aim of running them down, should never be volunteered.

Conduct towards Subordinates

Your success as an officer depends more on your conduct towards your subordinates, than anything else. The job of an officer is to take work from his subordinates and if he has acquired this knack, he is bound to be a very successful officer. You have to deal with hundreds of men and this is one of your most important jobs to ensure that each individual under you gives of his best. The result that you can produce depends on the work done by your subordinates. Alone you even if you are hard-working and sincere, will not be able to do much, if you are not able to enthuse your subordinates to work properly. For, no other government servant knows this technique of getting work from his subordinates, is so essential as for an executive officer.

The technique of human resource management consists of:

(a) team spirit;
(b) fairness and impartiality in your dealings;
(c) setting an example both in conduct and work;
(d) looking after the comforts of your men;
(e) solving the official difficulties of your subordinates; and
(f) encouraging the good workers and punishing the slackers for failure to do their work properly.

INTERRELATION OF PRIVATE LIFE AND OFFICIAL LIFE

There has been some conflict of opinion on this subject. On the one hand it has been suggested that the private life of a civil servant should be no concern of the State so long as his official duties are performed with devotion and integrity. The other view is that the private life of a civil servant must also be regulated by a rigid code of conduct; that is to say, a civil servant is not free to live and do as he pleases in his private life. Even when on leave he is expected to conduct himself with decorum and one view goes to the extent of requiring that even after his retirement a government servant has to behave in a responsible manner. This last view finds support from the fact that the continuance of the pension granted on retirement is subject to the pensioner's good conduct and behaviour and that it could be withheld if this condition is not fulfilled.

Private Life

The first view, namely, that a government servant's private life is his own affair, found sufficient votaries during the British regime. This was because an Indian was little concerned with the private life of the British official so long as he ruled well. It was immaterial whether he drank a full bottle of wine before retiring to bed or whether he kept odd company, and so on. For one thing, the majority of persons who came in contact with the British official knew little about his private life and cared still less about it. The English officials knew this and they could successfully live a life in private, quite separate from their official one.

A British civil servant at home, in England, did not enjoy so much freedom with respect to his private life as he did in India—there he was watched and his private life did have bearing on his official life.

The civil servants are now living in glass houses and their private activities are closely watched and subjected to comment. The averment that a civil servant's private life should be of little concern to the State takes it for granted that he can live a substandard life in his private apartment so long as his official work and duties are performed meticulously. This would have been all right if it were possible in the present conditions for a man to live two separate and independent lives:

(a) a standard life, and
(b) a substandard one.

But this is not humanly possible. The official duties of a person living a substandard life are bound to suffer just at standard milk suffers in quality when substandard milk is added to it. His prestige also suffers and with the loss of prestige there is also the loss of authority.

Critical Awareness of Parkinson's Laws

Most of the administrators would be aware of these laws, but many others may not be. These laws have stimulated a new line of thinking in administrative procedures and that is why a perusal of these laws puts the administrator on his guard against certain time-honoured practices which in the present times impede the efficient and speedy working of the administrative machinery.

In his famous propositions embodied in several volumes of Parkinson's Laws, Prof. C. Northcote Parkinson has propounded certain theories on the working of the administrative machinery in all modern governments. These theories have been evolved by him through a vast and costly research process. They are thought-provoking as they present ideas never debated before. They are of course true, though they have been written in a satirical style against the administrative systems prevailing in modern democracies.

Though produced in a previous chapter, it would not be out of place to discuss these laws, afresh for the benefit of readers.

His first law is that bureaucracy has a built-in capacity to grow and multiply, "Work expands to fill the time available for its completion" is Parkinson's first law. In support of this he quotes the proverb, "It is the busiest man who has time to spare."

The learned Professor illustrates his thesis by a short example: "Thus, an elderly lady of leisure can spend the entire day in writing and despatching a postcard... An hour will be spent in finding the postcard, another in hunting for spectacles, half an hour in a search for the address, an hour and a quarter in composition, and twenty minutes in deciding whether or not to take an umbrella when going to the pillar box in the next street. The total effort that would occupy a busy man for three minutes, all told, may in this fashion leave another person prostrate after a day of doubt, anxiety and toil".

It has been explained that work, specially paperwork, is this elastic in its demands on time, and that there is no relationship between the work to be done and the size of the staff to which it may be assigned.

In fact, the above law is the result of two motivating factors which are axiomatic—

(a) An officer wants to multiply subordinates, not rivals, and
(b) Officers make work for each other.

These and other factors have been discussed and elaborated by Parkinson in a light vein but realistic in substance.

Find out what the Country can Afford to Spend

Another law of Parkinson is that governmental expenditure rises to meet, and then exceed, the public revenue. He claims that this is a matter of the same everyday experience as his first law. When, for instance, an individual has a rise in his salary, he and his wife sit down to settle how the additional income is to be spent—so much on insurance, so much to be deposited in the savings bank, so much in the trust fund for the children. But no surplus ever comes their way. The extra salary disappears in extra expense. What is true of individuals is also true of governments. Whatever the revenue may be, there will always be the pressing need to spend it. The difference between a private individual and the government is that the government rarely pauses to consider what its income is. The learned professor then makes certain suggestions for the control of public expenditure, one being that ministers should begin not by ascertaining what their departments need but what the country can afford to spend. No department would be asked to submit an estimate; it will be given a fixed allocation within which to run itself.

The next step in his thesis is that a greatly reduced revenue would bring about an improvement, not a decline, in the public services. It is a paradox of administration that fewer people have less to do and, therefore, more time in which to think about what they are doing. When funds are limitless, the only economy made is in thinking. The worst inefficiencies do not arise from lack of funds but from a failure to decide what the object of spending is. It is this muddled thinking that leads to waste. Toward eliminating public waste the essential step is to reduce the total revenue. There will thus be less inclination to squander what is not there.

Law of Triviality

Another law about high finance which the professor has developed has been named by him as the Law of Triviality which means that the time spent on any item of the agenda of a finance committee will be in inverse proportion to the sum involved. That is to say the greater the sum, the lesser time is devoted to its consideration; the lesser the sum the greater the time devoted.

Though Prof. Parkinson does not say so, the same idea is expressed in the saying, 'penny wise, pound foolish'.

The learned professor has illustrated his theory in a sarcastic description of the proceedings of a meeting of a finance committee which included, among others, one item about approval for an atomic reactor estimated at £1,00,00,000 and another for an expenditure of £350 for constructing a bicycle shed. In a witty account Prof. Parkinson shows that the first-named item took some 2.30 minutes to pass whereas 45 minutes were spent in talks on the second.

The pettiest item was an estimate of £21 for refreshment supplied at meetings of the Joint Welfare Committee. It occupied an hour and a quarter after which the Secretary was asked to procure further information, leaving the matter to be decided at the next meeting.

The thing that accounts for this disparity is that while all the members knew a lot about refreshments and had something to contribute to the debate, a lesser number knew about the materials needed for the shed, its probable cost or the distinction between asbestos and galvanized iron which could be the alternative materials for its roof. And so far as the atomic reactor was concerned none had any idea except one member who thought it futile to make ignorant understand the intricacies of the project.

Among other things Prof. Parkinson is sarcastic about consultants and experts. In this connection he refers to the rule of safety and enunciates the precept that consultants and experts should be non-officials. This is because they will not have to carry the baby afterward and can always be trusted to give the kind of advice expected of them.

The following is an illustration taken from the description of Parkinson's Third Law: "The directors of the Horseless Carriage Company decided to streamline their organisation. They decided, therefore, to fire half the executives and demand some real work from the other half. Their problem was how to do this without being tarred and feathered in the middle of the Company's parking plot. In order to avoid this they agreed that their proposed reorganisation should be the work of outside consultants. So they called in Messrs Snearing, Stockwell and Foggarty and explained briefly what advice they expected to receive. In such a situation as this, the consultant's chief advantage is that he need not linger on the scene. He presents the report with one foot in the jet aircraft's door, reaching 20,000 feet before any one has finished reading the first paragraph which consists entirely of thanks to all for their co-operation."

The following is a list of the results achieved in the process of 'streamlining' on their recommendations:

(a) Half the executives were fired.
(b) A digital computer costing $10,00,000 was acquired as a symbol of progress.
(c) All partitions were demolished, making a general office out of the space previously occupied by individual officers.
(d) The office colour scheme which had been primrose and white was changed to lilac and grey.

Administrator's Difficulty in Applying Sound Administrative Principles

A serious handicap from which the Indian administrator suffers is the low level of social efficiency and honesty. The result is that the bulk of the civil services are manned by persons who are substandard in discipline, orderliness and devotion to duty. Further, the stress on economic life amongst the persons of that class makes it difficult for them to resist the temptation of easy money. In the words of *Daily Pioneer*, "No administrator can have a higher standard of morality of efficiency than the country's general level of social efficiency or honesty. Corruption, it has been said, is a result of inadequate public morality. It has also a certain close relationship with the degree of economic prosperity that a society has attained. That is one reason why the same administrative system produces more corruption in a State like ... than in a State like ... Often corruption comes from the public's attempt to get results at the speed it wants instead of at the speed which is convenient to the official".

It is in these circumstances that a handful of administrators finds it almost impossible to check corruption is spite of numerous government directives in this regard. There is another handicap which was equally and effectively pinpointed in the same editorial article of *The Pioneer*. That handicap arises from the direct relationship between the level of administrative efficiency and honesty on the one hand and the level of social efficiency and honesty on the other.

OFFICER'S COMPANION

Fortunately for us, the ideal of a Welfare State is not in our country, it is a controversial political issue; it is the goal laid down in the Constitution itself. Far from being a neutralist, the public servant of today, and still more of tomorrow, should be one rich in human sympathy and with a fully awakened social conscience. To his work he must bring not only competence but faith and fervour and a mind, receptive as well as constructive, able to see beyond the immediate difficulties the opportunities that lie ahead.

Administrators and Politicians should Interact Amiably

We have then the observations of Sri H.V.R. Iyengar, another distinguished member of the ICS, since retired, dealing with the relations between ministers and administrative officers. "As the old guard disappears", he says, "future ministers may be men not merely without administrative experience but without the romantic halo of political suffering, and it is particularly important that, for regulating relations between them and the permanent officials, sound conventions should be established. The solution does not lie in purely structural devices, in any 'organization and methods' directives, but in a realignment of the mutual attitude of ministers and officials. Basically, this means that, while it is clearly understood that the ministers are the deciding authorities and that their decision must be given effect to, it is the right and duty of the officials frankly and fearlessly to advise: this means that such frankness is appreciated and encouraged rather than frowned upon, and that, in general, both sides respect each other. This is putting it in very simple form, of course, for respect transcends the mere recognition of spheres of authority; it extends to the field of character, which is another matter."

The same idea has been propounded by John Pliffner in these words: "The realisation of the fact that politics and administration cannot always be separated and isolated should not vitiate the basic soundness of a gentleman's agreement that one will not encroach upon the other in a meddlesome manner. The success to be attained in this direction will depend largely upon the extent to which partisan politics is kept out of administration. This will entail just as great an obligation for the administrative personnel to abstain from political controversy as for the politicians to keep hands off administration."

The Democratic Spirit

For a full-fledged democracy there are several requirements such as:

(i) A democratic constitution—democracy not in outward form, but in its fullest scope and spirit.

(ii) The political parties through whom the constitution is worked—both the party in power and the parties in opposition—have, in their organization, to function as pure democratic units. A party with a dictatorial sort of organization would not bring a true spirit of democracy to its functioning if put in charge of political power.

(iii) The electorate too should be democratic minded.

(iv) Not the least important is the factor that the public services should have a democratic bearing and a democratic outlook to be able to serve democratic statesmen representing the party in power and deal properly with the parties in opposition.

ELEVEN

PRINCIPLES OF CONDUCT RULES

The conduct rules are really an elaboration of the all-embracing word 'duty' in relation to civil service servants. They lay down broad propositions on the following:

(a) how duty is to be well performed, and

(b) what things are to be shunned or avoided so that there may be no blot on the proper performance of his duties by the civil servant.

Principles of All-India Conduct Rules

Thus, for instance, the All-India Service (Conduct) Rules 1954, lay down:

(i) That a member of an All-India Service "shall at all times maintain absolute integrity and devotion to duty" —Rule 3.

(ii) That it "shall be the duty of every member of the service to endeavour to prevent any member of his family from taking part in, subscribing in aid of or assisting in any other manner any movement or activity which is or tends directly or indirectly to be, subversive of the Government as by law established...."—Rule 4, sub-section 2.

(iii) "A member of the service shall so manage his private affairs as to avoid habitual indebtedness or insolvency. A member of the service who becomes the subject of a legal proceeding for insolvency shall forthwith report the full facts to the Government.."—Rule 14.

The tenor of the rules is to point out the nature of duty under a given set of circumstances. They contain a narration of many 'don'ts together with some affirmative rules. Both the positive as well as the negative rules are intended to secure the doing of duty.

The word 'duty' in the abstract sense is difficult to comprehend; therefore, these rules aim at particularising certain matters as indicative of that abstract notion.

The Basic Principles of Conduct

In this context the basic principles of conduct may be stated as below:

I. Life is inseparable from service. There is no possibility of escape from service.
II. In the ultimate analysis, every service turns to service of mankind. Service of self is also service to humanity.
III. Human happiness is related to service which well-performed.
IV. Service can be well performed by doing it with devotion.
V. The better performance of service also requires adherence to a set of regulations which have been evolved by long experience by those who have excelled in the art of better service. In relation to government service regulations are the 'Government Servants' Conduct Rules'.

The Necessity of Conduct Rules

All professions and trades have their rules of conduct. For the legal practitioners there are rules of professional conduct, so also for the physician and the surgeon. The sportsperson has also a set of rules to abide by, and the businessperson too. All are bound by their code of conduct which they so scrupulously follow. It is thus in the fitness of things that we have a set of rules governing the conduct and behaviour of public servants. Since government service is not an autonomous profession, it is all the more necessary that there should be effective rules for the civil services.

The rules for civil servants differ from the code of professional conduct of autonomous professions, e.g. law, medicine in the binding nature of the obligations. While in the case of the professions, the observance of the rules largely depends upon the morale of the professional, the rules for the services are absolute and any breach thereof is punishable in disciplinary proceedings. Thus, there is the element of compulsion in the case of the services.

Importance of the Rules

Amongst the rules regulating the conditions of service of civil servants, the most important are the Conduct Rules. Government expects every civil servant to make himself familiar with them and also to observe them with sincerity. A breach of any of these rules amounts to misconduct which is punishable in disciplinary proceedings by dismissal, removal, demotion (major punishments) or by stoppage of annual increments or by censure or by any of the other minor punishments.

The Uttar Pradesh Disciplinary Proceedings Enquiry Committee had occasion to draw attention to the fact that government servants were not as mindful of the provisions of the Government Servants' Conduct Rules as they used to be in the past although in 1948 copies of the rules had been supplied to all gazetted officers in order to make them aware of their obligations under the rules. The State Government agreed with this observation and issued circular instructions that all gazetted officers in the State should acquire full knowledge of the provisions of these Rules 13 and 14 relating respectively with public demonstrations in honour of officers and presentation of trowels, etc. at ceremonial functions. It was emphasized that these rules should be strictly enforced and a warning was added that parties held in violation of these rules amounted to a breach thereof.

Historical Retrospect

Mention may first be made of a typical verse in *Kiratarjuniyam*, the great Sanskrit work by the poet Bharavi, in which a general indication has been given of the primary duty of a Civil Servant. Therein it is stated that an official should always and in all circumstances tell his superior officers that which he himself believes to be a fact without fear or favour. He should never twist facts in order that his account may be pleasing to his superior. Such a course could not be in the best interest of the public servant. Sometimes truth may be bitter but still there are advantages in the truthful course. Words, which at the same time are as sweet as beneficial, are rare.

The instructions given in the *Arthashastra* of Kautilya (Chanakya) will also be found interesting in as much as they lay down some useful principles for the conduct of government servants. The English rendering is as follows:

(a) "With such agreements with the king, he (a courtier) may enter on the duty assigned to him. He shall sit by the side of, and close to the king and far from the seat of another courtier. He shall avoid speaking slyly against the opinion of any member of the assembly; he shall never make incredible or false statements; nor loud laughter with no cause for jest and loud noise and spurt. He shall also avoid talking to another in secret, mutual conversation with another in the assembly (of ministers), appearing in royal dress in the public, haughtiness, buffoonery, open request for gains and promotions, seeing with one eye, biting the lips, brow-beating, interrupting the king while speaking, enmity with a strong party, association with women, pimps, messages of foreign kings, enemies, inimical parties, dismissed officers and wicked people, stubborn adherence to a single purpose and contact with any confederacy of men.

(b) "When asked, he should tell the king what is both good and pleasing but what is not bad, though pleasing; if the king is pleased to listen, he may secretly tell what, though unpleasant, is good.

"While laughing in jest, he shall avoid loud laughter; he shall avoid evil aspersions against others, nor ascribe them to others; he shall forgive evil done to himself and have much forbearance as the earth."

Historical Review of the Conduct Rules during the British Regime

During their long administration of India, the British implanted many things in the country that were done in England. During the early part of the rule of the East India Company, the servants of the company had a free hand in almost everything. The Rules of Conduct as we now have them were unknown. The practice of purchase of resignations and consequential purchase of appointments was rampant. Thus, a prospective appointee paid a settled sum to an official as price for his resigning office.

Simultaneously, he paid another sum to the appointing authority as price for his appointment to the post thus vacated. Likewise, an office falling vacant in the normal course went to him who offered the highest price. This was what was happening in England too where there were almost open bids for the purchase of an office under the Crown. In fact, some of the Company's higher officers came to India by purchasing their appointments. Of course, there had been some half-herded efforts by the Company to control the morale of its servants by requiring them to give up certain indiscriminate practices which were injurious to the Company's interests. For instance, in 1842 a general notification was issued prohibiting the Company's servants in purchasing of resignations. Such instructions were, however, of a rudimentary character and there was nothing in them which would be equated to the conduct rules as we now have them.

Things began to improve when following the first war of Indian Independence, the administration of India was taken over by the British Crown in 1858, Queen Victoria being the reigning sovereign then. It was in the same year that the first instruction regarding the conduct of the Queen's officers in India was issued and it related to the prohibition in the acquisition of property by European officers without the prior permission of the government. Then in 1876 it was laid down, as a directive, that without the previous sanction of the government no officer in India shall accept any gift or gratuity or reward from any Indian. This was almost the first prohibition which had the colour of a conduct rule.

This directive was followed in 1885 by another directive against private trade or employment by a government servant. During the Company's reign everybody's salary was very low and at the same time the means of making money by private trade or employment were immense. Even during the Crown's administration private trade by government was quite prevalent and it was not until the above stated year that this practice was banned absolutely. Gift could, of course, be accepted conditionally, that was on the condition that government sanctioned their acceptance but private trade was completely abolished. Now and then certain other instructions were issued and it was in 1962 that these various instructions which had become quite sizeable by then, were given shape. They were collected together and given the name of Government Servants' Conduct Rules. They had the authority of the Governor-General who was paramount throughout India, the provincial administrations having very limited powers. These were not published separately but formed part of the manual of government orders which contained administrative instructions of all kinds. It was much afterwards that the Conduct Rules were published separately.

Evolution of the Rules

The Conduct Rules of 1902 were a common set of rules applicable to all government servants in India. They were brought up-to-date in 1935 and were issued under the name of Government Servants' Conduct Rules, 1935. Then, in 1942 separate rules were issued for the Secretary of State's Services under the name of Secretary of State's of State under sections 247(1), 250 and 269 of the Government of India Act, 1935. By these rules, the Government Servants' (Conduct) Rules, 1935, were cancelled insofar as they were applicable to the Secretary of State's services.

Various Sets of Conduct Rules

There are now in existence several sets of Conduct Rules such as the following:

(i) For services under the rule-making control of the President:

(a) Secretary of State's Services (Conduct) Rules, 1942. These are applicable to members of the Secretary of State's Services, such as the Indian Civil Services, the Indian Police Service, the Indian Service of Engineers, the Indian Forest Service, the Indian Education Service. These services are getting gradually finished and their place has been taken by the All-India Services.

(b) All-India Services (Conduct) Rules, 1968 have been framed by the President under article 309 of the Constitution and are applicable to the members of All-India Services such as the Indian Administrative Service, the Indian Police Service, the Indian Forest Service, the Indian Service of Engineers, the Indian Foreign Service. These rules of 1968 have replaced the earlier rules of 1954.

(c) Central Civil Services (Conduct) Rules, 1964

(d) Railway Services (Conduct) Rules.

(ii) For services under the rule-making control of the Governor:

(a) Government Servants' Conduct Rules of general applicability in each State.

(b) Conduct Rules for special classes of civil services in some of the States.

The rules of the various services are common in essential matters with minor variations in particular details.

Study of Some Rules

The All-India Services (Conduct) Rules, 1958, contain the basic principles for the conduct and behaviour of civil servants in general though by their terms they are applicable only to members of the All-India Services. A couple of these rules are discussed below:

Misconduct in Private Life

Rule 3 of the All India Rules is relevant in this connection. It lays down that every member of an All-India Service 'shall at all times maintain absolute integrity and devotion to duty'. Now, 'absolute integrity and devotion to duty' is not possible for an official who misconducts himself in private life. For the proper observance to this rule, therefore, it is necessary that the officer's private life should also be free from blemish. In this connection there is a rule of the Allahabad High Court in which it has been held that an officer can be punished by dismissal, removal or otherwise for misconduct in private life.

Unauthorised Communication of Information

Rule 9 of the All-India rules deals with this subject. According to it, a member of an All-India Service shall not communicate any official document or information to any government servant or to any other person to whom he is not authorised to communicate such document or information, provided that this prohibition shall not apply when he is acting under some general or special order of government or is performing in good faith his assigned duties.

A classic example of the application of the principle of this rule will be found in an incident in the last days of the life of Peshwa

Madhav Rao I who died at the early age of 27 in 1772 after having ruled for 11 years. He suffered from a long and painful illness in the form of tuberculosis of the intestines for which there was no known remedy at that time. Still his administration was most efficient up to the very last hour of his life. The awareness of approaching end did not disturb his composure of mind. As days went by, the pain in his stomach so increased that he asked his attendants to finish his life. Devoid of all appetite, he nevertheless forced himself to take something to prevent others from going without food. Having lost hope of recovery he began to destroy a stock of secret papers he had about him. One of his ministers humbly questioned the propriety of his action. Whereupon, the Peshwa asked him to take out a certain bundle from a nearby chest, to read its contents and to say whether it should be destroyed or preserved. The minister was surprised to find that the papers related to his own intrigues. As a seasoned statesman, the Peshwa had never given this minister any occasion even to suspect that he was holding proofs against the minister's guilt. He was well aware of his good qualities too and did not wish to dismiss him. Now, he was destroying those proofs so that after his death they might not fall into the hands of unauthorised and unscrupulous persons who might use them against the minister for their personal motives.

The tribute paid to this sagacious ruler by the historian Sir Richard Temple will be read with interest: "In his love for the justice, he paid compensation to the ryots for the loss caused by the troops. He undertook tours to make personal enquiries into the grievances of his subjects and took prompt measures to redress them. As a remarkable administrator and fearless general, he more than made good the loss which the Maratha prestige had suffered on the disaster of Panipat. Dying in the full bloom of youth, Madhav Rao has left behind the reputation of being one of the finest characters that the Indian nationality has produced."

Indebtedness

Rule 15 of the All-India Rules requires a member of an All-India Service to manage his private affairs as to avoid habitual indebtedness or insolvency. A similar rule occurs in other sets of rules too. This is based on a sound principle of public policy. Thus, when a court order is issued attaching a part of a civil servant's salary towards the satisfaction of his debt, a slur is cast upon him and he feels an inferiority complex in the presence of his colleagues. Financial embarrassment also leads to frequent absence from duty either to avoid the visits of creditors or to obtain protection from the court under insolvency enactments. The case of England vis-a-vis indebtedness is that pecuniary embarrassment is punished with penalties of varying severity according to the culpability of the office from loss of promotion or annual increment to more severe punishment. Suspension from duty and salary is imposed for debt or bankruptcy, and reinstatement is possible if it is found that the civil servant's difficulties had been caused by unavoidable misfortune. Failure to inform the head of his department that he has been arrested for debt or that he had applied to the court for insolvency might cause removal from service.

As early as 1842, the British Board of Stamps and Taxes made the following observations on the subject:

> "An efficient performance of his official duty is not to be expected from any person involved in pecuniary difficulties as the time and thoughts of such a person, instead of being engaged in his official business, must necessarily be occupied in constant effort to meet the exigencies of the day and further it is highly inexpedient that any officer in such circumstances should be placed in a position of trust".
>
> Further, "The public have right to expect that a high moral standard should be maintained by the executive of Government with reference to all civil servants of Her Majesty and especially those filling the higher situations."

This is what Mr. George Hamilton, Permanent Secretary to the British Treasury (Finance Department) wrote to the Stationery Office on 11-5-1861. He explained to Mr. William E. Gladstone, the Chancellor of Exchequer (Finance Minister) that the Treasury's task was to preserve and reinforce that morality. The Treasury's concern to uphold the morality of the service and to prevent it suffering from 'the unworthiness of some of its members' was inspired partly by considerations of efficiency. An officer in financial difficulty cannot be an efficient officer.

Transactions Regarding Property

Restrictions about acquisition and disposal of property are contained in Rule 16 of the All-India Rules. According to it transactions by a member of an All-India service in respect of movable or immovable property have in certain cases to be reported to Government while for some others previous sanction of Government is needed for the contemplated transaction.

It might interest the readers to be informed that the prohibition against sale or purchase of property by civil servants of the British Crown in India has been in force from 1858, that is immediately following the First War of Indian Independence in 1857 and the assumption by the Crown of direct responsibility for Indian affairs. The administration of India had then been taken over from the East India Company by the British Government and the servants of the Company became the servants of the Throne of England.

The prohibition was the result of the sale of a house by a public officer to an Indian gentleman. The officer, who was serving under the Government of Bengal, had with the cognizance of his immediate superior officer, sold a house to an Indian gentleman living within his jurisdiction for Rs. 90/-. There was not even the remotest reason to suppose that the sale was in any respect otherwise than a fair transaction. However, in due course the matter came to the notice of the Court Directors through a report from the Indian Government whereupon the Court directed in a despatch dated 4-3-1858 that sale of this description between public servants in India and Indians within their jurisdiction should be strictly prohibited. This decision was published in the Government of India Gazette notification No. 4011 issued by the President-in-Council in the Foreign Department dated December 3, 1858. The idea underlying this prohibition will be evident from the portion of the notification herein reproduced: "The President-in-Council is assured that pecuniary transactions of an objectionable nature between public servants and natives of India seldom, if any, now occur and had the fullest reverence of the honour of the British Throne's servants in all departments, but transactions of the nature alluded to, though in themselves entirely fair and perfectly free from both sides from all unworthy motives, are liable to being misconstrued and when misconstrued, are no less mischievous in their effect than corrupt dealings. In conformity, therefore, with instructions of the Hon'ble Court all such sales are prohibited. Should a public officer be doubtful whether a transaction to which he desires to become a party comes within this prohibition, he will consult his superior officer and be guided by the instructions he may receive. A controlling officer consulted on such an occasion will dispose of the case himself or refer it for orders of the Government as he may consider proper".

Conduct Rules vis-a-vis Fundamental Rights

In 1952, the Government of India had occasion to consider the question whether the provisions in the Government Servants' Conduct Rules violated the Fundamental Rights guaranteed under the Constitution. After consulting the Union Ministry of Law, the Home Ministry explained the position to the State Governments in these terms:

1. "It is necessary to emphasise that the relationship between the Government and a civil servant rests on contractual basis. In some case the contract is evidenced by a formal document, but even where there is no formal document, there is nonetheless a contract implied by the conduct of the parties. The provisions of the Constitution and the various rules (and the residuary power of the Government to alter those rules) together comprise the terms and conditions of that contract of service and define the rights, duties and obligations of the Government on the one hand and the civil servant on the other. A person who voluntarily enters government service, therefore, accepts these rules and conditions voluntarily in his own interest. The Government Servants' Conduct Rules, moreover, have reference exclusively to the duration of this contract. Any breach of these rules is punishable at worst by his removal from service. The restrictions imposed by the rules are not in truth and substance imposed upon him externally, but he accepts and abides by them voluntarily in his own interest. The operation of these rules, therefore, cannot be said to be an invasion of any of the fundamental rights. If the civil servant does not exercise these fundamental rights to the fullest, he does so merely because he considers it in his

interest not to do so. But it is open to him at any time to exercise his fundamental right by resigning from the civil service. He has no fundamental rights to insist that he should be retained in government service and that he should have the benefit of all the rights and privileges of the contract of service if, on his own part, he does not abide by his own obligations and duties arising from that very contract.

2. "In the contrary view, every contract of service necessarily involves the invasion of fundamental rights of the civil servants and other employees in many ways. For instance, the contract of service of a civil servant (as indeed of any other employee) requires him to devote his time and energy to the discharge of his official functions and so preclude him from engaging himself in any other trade or profession; it likewise requires his presence at his place of duty for specified period and so precludes him from going to other places during the periods; and by analogy of the arguments advanced by the Governments of Assam and Orissa every such contract of service would involve invasion of the fundamental rights of the employee under sub-clauses (g) and (d) of clause (1) of Article 19. The views suggested by these Governments would lead to the conclusion that Article 19 would have the effect to invalidate every contract of employment under a government or a public authority, etc. A view leading to such absurd results cannot be sustained."

The Government of India was ıurther advised that the above position was not affected by the presence, in Part III of the Constitution, of Article 33 which expressly authorises Parliament by law to restrict or abrogate any of the fundamental rights in the case of the armed forces, etc. The inclusion of that article was necessary because maintenance of discipline among members of these services necessarily and frequently required action in contravention of certain provision of Part III of the Constitution—for instance, detention otherwise that in accordance with Article 21 and the liability to be tried and punished by court martial as well as by ordinary courts.

For these reasons the Government of India held the opinion

that the provisions in the Conduct Rules which place any restrictions on the freedom of speech and expression of government servants and on their right to form associations are not inconsistent with the provisions of the Constitution. The Government of India also added that a relevant point in this connection was that even in the United States civil servants were prohibited from taking part in politics and it has never been suggested that the prohibition involves any encroachment on any fundamental right.

The Unwritten Code of Conduct

Supplement to the Conduct Rules which are statutory rules, or to be precise, constitutional rules (that is rules made under Article 309 of the Constitution), there are certain accepted propositions on the conduct of civil servants in general. These are in the form of time-honoured principles which, though not resting on statutory authority, are nevertheless treated as axiomatic. They have been put down in precise terms in the Report of Board of Inquiry which has been set-up by the Government of United Kingdom, the report being published in 1978. The principles set out in it received the approval of the Government. The relevant portions of the report explain in clear terms what is expected of a civil servant and how he should shape his conduct in matters in which his duty and his private interests are in conflict and in his relation to the public.

In this context the following verse adds to the meaning:

> *A wise man will so act that whatever he does may rather seem voluntary and of his own free will than done by compulsion, however much he may be compelled by necessity.*
>
> MACHIAVELLI

TWELVE

RULES OF CONDUCT FOR GOVERNMENT OFFICERS

The whole thesis of official conduct and behaviour is founded upon duty which is well performed. This proposition has been verified by E.S. Hooper in the following couplet:

'I slept and dreamt that life was beauty;
I worked and found that life was duty.'

This is the pivot upon which rests the whole body of conduct rules and conventions for civil servants. A perusal of the rules will show how aptly these lines fit in with the conduct required of a civil servant. So far as the rules, distinguished from conventions are concerned, they are binding on the civil servant with the pain of disciplinary action for their breach. The conventions, on the other hand, have no statutory authority but it is in the interest of the officer himself to abide by them so that he may be safe from criticism or even departmental action. The verse quoted also embodies the spirit underlying the conduct rules, and this spirit is more important than the text of the rules. If an officer imbibes this spirit, then he can never be called upon to answer a charge of the breach of any of the rules.

Conduct in Official Behaviour

In August 1958, during the Chief Ministership of Dr. Sampurnanand, the U.P. Government gave thought to the subject of the conduct of civil servants in their relations with the public or in the discharge of their duties. As a result, certain basic propositions were formulated to remind the officers of their responsibility in this matter. These were put in the form of *Aide Memoire of Official Behaviour* which was circulated to all Heads of Departments, Commissioners of Divisions and other administrative officers with a demi-official letter from the Chief Secretary.

A year later, as a result of certain incidents brought to government's notice, it became necessary to supplement those propositions and this was done by the issue of a supplement to the said *Aide Memoire*.

The conduct of civil servants, it was stated in the *Aide Memoire* had become a subject of frequent discussion. Instances had come to the government in the form of direct complaints from members of public or through reports from senior administrative officers. Not unoften, the matter was also discussed in the legislature.

Government did, of course, realise that this criticism was often exaggerated; sometimes it was entirely baseless. At the same time, it was felt that, on occasions, an officer behaved in an unbecoming manner giving rise to valid resentment. Since the attainment of independence, the functions of civil officers had greatly changed, leading the public to entertain high expectations from the official machinery. Complaints and criticism frequently caused disappointment, when the officials in government departments failed to rise up to the expectation of the public.

The government had been viewing the whole question with an uneasy feeling. While there was no intention to give credence to irresponsible criticism, it was felt that widespread and sustained criticism of the conduct of administrative officers tend to undermine their usefulness and shake the trust of the public in the governmental machinery. In these circumstances, it was considered necessary to call attention to certain broad principles which should regulate the behaviour of civil officers towards the public and their conduct in discharging of their duties properly. It was with this end the *Aide Memoire* and its supplement were issued.

In the original *Aide Memoire*, followed by its supplement, the various propositions were grouped under a number of short descriptive headings. In the supplement *Memoire* there were certain points on matters covered by the original *Memoire* as well as a couple of new subjects. These have been suitably amalgamated in the following paragraphs in order to give a comprehensive idea of the entire subject.

Dealings with the Public

Members of the public are becoming increasingly conscious of their rights. It is essential for any administration to ensure that the public have full trust in the officers of the government. Apart from incorruptibility, which has been dealt with in the last paragraph, efficiency and proper behaviour are the two essential requirements of a civil servant. By their actions the interests of the common men are badly affected. Civil servants should, therefore, constantly bear in mind that the common man has a right to expect not only that his affairs are dealt with effectively and expeditiously but also that his personal feelings, not less than his right, are sympathetically and fairly considered. Delay in the disposal of public business is a general ground of complaint and a positive approach has to be made at all levels to ascertain the causes of delay and to remove them.

Another consideration in dealing with the public is the show of courtesy. A citizen may have a, however, humble status in society, expects to be dealt with courteously and to be heard patiently. An attitude of superiority towards him does not help. It merely creates a sense of bitterness which is not good for the administration. Courtesy always pays even if it is not dictated by detailed rules of official etiquette which has thus been expressed by the fact.

Incorruptibility

Allegations of corruption against civil servants are widespread. Though many of these are exaggerated and some are not more than mere generalisations, it is necessary that an effective drive should be launched by not only every head of the department but also every head of the office to ensure that the officials under him adopt clean methods and are scrupulous in the discharge of their duties. It is possible that the level at which the public largely come in contact with the official machinery, there is a show of authority, lack of understanding and even corruption in the ranks. There is the need for introspection about this on the part of every one and administrative officers have to satisfy themselves that they are making positive efforts against raising corruption charges against them.

The necessity of eradicating corruption cannot be overemphasized. Apart from the obvious forms, corruption can take many other forms. For example, some officers do not make their own lodging arrangements and stay with their subordinates while on tour. This practice directly or indirectly leads to corruption and must be discouraged strongly. To expect a low-paid subordinate to accommodate his superior officer and to feed him lavishly, is to open the way for corruption. Additionally, this makes the officer obligatory to his own subordinates and thus restrict his ability to deal strictly with the cases of inefficiency, indiscipline or corruption that may come to the officer's knowledge. The importance of integrity in administration was emphasized in a short broadcast by Dr. Sampurnanand, the then Chief Minister of the state, on 12th February, 1957.

Misuse of Official Position

Closely allied to corruption is the misuse of official position by an officer. There had been cases in which an officer on tour or recess had his departmental office vacated so as to use the vacated accommodation for his own family members or relatives. Another case was of an officer who requisitioned a jeep from his subordinate from a long distance so that he could use it for local journeys at a particular station where he was staying. Such conduct is considered as most reprehensible by the government.

Avoidance of Personal Publicity

Magazines, booklets, etc., published by various departments often contain a profusion of photographs of government officers. Criticism has rightly been directed against this practice. Public funds are not to be utilized for personal publicity of officers. These magazines, booklets, etc. will serve their purpose better if they describe the activities of the government. Even in cases where departmental work is to be narrated, it would be preferable to lay greater emphasis on the achievements of the department rather than on departmental officers. It is for the administrative officers to ensure that all officers under them understand this point which was advocated in the second D.O. also wherein it was emphasized that an officer should avoid personal publicity in his work and all forms of ostentation in public behaviour. As an example, the case was cited of a head of department who, on his way to the station where he was to recess, was received at different places laying on the route by ten individual officers of his department each of whom showed his journey as on tour and charged travelling allowance. In another case, the head of a department had traffic stopped for him when he was passing through certain areas and who was received and garlanded at several places en-route. The government expressed their condemnation of such conduct.

The conduct of officers in laying foundation-stones or in inaugurating public functions should also be regulated on these grounds. It will add to the effectiveness of an officer if he endeavours to function in anonymity. It is, of course, not intended that he should not be present at such functions. Actually, participation in them, wherever possible and convenient, would be helpful in as much as his presence is likely to add to the enthusiasm of the people and help them in their difficulties. An officer should, however, not accept the leading role in such functions.

Interdepartmental Harmony

There is much greater need for interdepartmental co-ordination and goodwill today than ever before. The functions and responsibilities of government are now much more broad-based. It is impossible for the administrative machinery to work in watertight compartments. There is need for complete coordination and collaboration amongst the departments. Interdepartmental 'superiorities' and estrangements become a source of embarrassment to government and hinder the orderly conduct of public business. They also invite ridicule from the public. Differences of opinion can be settled at proper levels with the help of senior officers. But there is neither need to have talk of them in the public nor should the governmental business be allowed to suffer on that account.

Detachment from Political Parties

For the proper discharge of his duties, an officer must take a live interest in the social and economic affairs of the country and it is not intended that he should live in a vacuum. At the same time an officer has to conduct himself properly in his work and conversation in such a way as to leave no room for an impression that he has any alignment with any political party. An officer whose duty is to deal with the public has to make himself accessible to all and to deal with them with patience and courtesy and in doing justice. In short, an officer is expected to take an objective view of things, a view which is unconnected with the ideologies of any particular political party. Civil servants at all levels should be made aware of this.

Discipline and Restraint in Conversation

There is a tendency on the part of civil servants towards irresponsible talk concerning the affairs of government. In such talk, personal remarks are sometimes made against political parties, members of government and senior officers. Such talk is derogatory to the prestige, position and reputation of the official who indulges in it, apart from the fact that it is an act of indiscipline and is directly opposed to the Government Servant's Conduct Rules. A person who does not show respect for those in authority can never expect to command the respect of his levels. Such people are expected to behave with a sense of responsibility in the matter of discussion and conversation by exercising the utmost restraint and care. A senior officer can also make his contribution towards the checking of the falling standards of discipline in all spheres of life by himself adhering to the rules of discipline and thus setting an example. The word 'discipline' is being used here in its wider sense of orderliness, methodical way of doing things, consideration for others and so on. In this sense, unpunctuality, slovenly behaviour and the like would amount to acts of indiscipline. Civil officers are expected to be a disciplined body exhibiting better standards of behaviour than others.

Recreation

Government realises that civil servants, like other hardworking people, should take part in some recreational activities. Recreation adds to efficiency and health. While everyone is free to select his own form of recreation, there is one general consideration which has to be kept in mind. It is to be ensured that no officer places himself under any obligation to another person in this matter. There are persons who form motives of self-interest are ready to oblige officials but the same persons are likely to turn up some day with an unfair request. All recreation should, therefore, be at only one's expense, or among friends on a reciprocal basis.

Reception of Criticism

Some officers are inclined to take criticism to heart with a resulting feeling of despondency while some others are entirely impervious to criticism. No approach is correct. Criticism has its value if seen in a proper perspective that is to say if it is received with an objective approach by subordinating personal feelings even though the criticism may have been expressed in personal terms. If the criticised officer finds that there is room for improvement, on his part, he should welcome the criticism as a reminder for him to change his attitude. On the other hand, if he finds that the criticism is baseless, he need not give a second thought to it. At the same time, he should avoid a feeling of animosity against his critic. If, however, the matter commented upon requires public denial or clarification, the officer should take prompt steps to do so or, if necessary, refer it to the government for orders. It is this way that criticism can be turned to the advantage of the public service.

Good Manners

The government have noted certain instances of the decline in good manners on the part of their officers with regret in some distinguished persons. In others, while the officer had received an invitation for himself, he brought, with him, members of his family who had not been invited. It was also noticed that these officers were not properly dressed. The functions were of a formal character in honour of visiting dignitaries and those invited were expected to come suitably dressed. A lack of punctuality was also noticed. Some officers came even after the arrival of the chief guest. Some other left the function before the departure of the chief guest. Small courtesies usually extended to an honoured guest were disregarded. For instance, some officers started eating before the chief guest began, while some other were talking and laughing loudly in the immediate vicinity of the distinguished guests.

These lapses, in their cumulative effect, give the impression of a lack of good manners and were noted with deep regret by the members of government. Civil officers have the advantage of training and discipline which is unavailable to the public in general. A much higher standard of discipline is expected from government officers in official and social spheres. Much depends upon the attitude of senior officers and the example they set. The supplemental *Aide Memoire* also dealt with the subject of appropriate dress to be worn by civilian officers on different occasions. This matter has been dealt with in subsequent chapters.

Consumption of Alcoholic Drinks in Public

The supplemental *Aide Memoire* drew attention to two earlier circulars, in which the policy of government regarding the consumption of alcoholic drinks by civil servants, was laid down. The supplement then went on to say that it had been stated in those circulars that the prohibition of consumption, except for medicinal purposes, of intoxicating drinks injurious to health, has been incorporated in the "Directive Principles of State Policy" in the Constitution and that, although government had no desire to interfere with the private life of any citizen, it expected that civil servants wish to exercise the necessary restraint upon themselves to lead a clean life and to conduct themselves in conformity with the principles underlying the State Government's policy of prohibition. The following points were then emphasized:

(a) Where total prohibition has been introduced in any part of the State, public servants are, like all other citizens, subject to the prohibition laws and must not make use of alcoholic drink. They are also expected to set an example to other citizens. A public servant contravening prohibition laws is liable to departmental disciplinary action in addition to such other actions, as may be considered necessary, to take in a court of law.

(b) Even where prohibition has not been introduced, civil officers are expected, by their personal conduct, to set an example for others to follow. The policy of government is that civil servants should avoid the use of intoxicants and abstain from taking any alcoholic drinks in public. Drinking in hotels, bars, pubs and restaurants is considered to be drinking in public.

In this connection, rule 4-A of the U.P. Government Servants' Conduct Rules is also relevant. The portion concerned runs:

Drinking

Subject to the provisions of any law relating to intoxicating drinks or drugs for the time being, in force, in any area, no government servant shall:

(a) while on duty be under the influence of such drinks or drugs to such an extent as to render him incapable of discharging his duty properly and efficiently, or

(b) appear in a public place in a state of intoxication, or

(c) habitually use such drinks or drugs in excess.

Rule 20 of the All- India Services (Conduct) Rules, 1958 is also in the same terms.

For misconduct under this rule, it is sufficient if the government servant moves at a public place in a state of intoxication. The government has the power to prohibit government servants from taking intoxicating drinks in social functions as well.

Opinion within the Services

The *Aide Memoire* points out that civil servants are apt to forget the value of traditions within the services. Healthy traditions must be set by senior officers so that there may be a sort of public opinion within their own ranks which will discountenance on lapses on the part of individual officer. Fear of losing face among colleagues is a more effective deterrent than the fear of departmental punishment. The government expressed the hope that all right-thinking officers would help to create the correct opinion within the services.

Always Remember

In the end the *Aide Memoire* stated that it was impossible to draw up a catalogue of the manner in which public servants should act in the discharge of their duties. Only the more important principles could be mentioned. In matters uncovered by the text of the *Aide Memoire*, the officers will have to decide for themselves how best to act or to conduct themselves in the situations that arise in day-to-day administration. In doing so, the officers will realise that it is their privilege to serve the interests of the people and that every privilege carries a corresponding responsibility with it. An officer should also remember that his conduct is to be so ordered that it assures, in terms of the preamble to the Constitution, "the dignity of the individual and the unity of the nation."

It was also explained that the instructions in the *Aide Memoire* were likely to make some encroachment on the private conduct of officers. While government had no intention to interfere unduly in the private lives of their employees, it was to be realised that in a welfare state, government activities embrace almost every sphere of human life resulting in continuous association of civil servants with the public. Therefore, it was difficult to demarcate public conduct from private behaviour. The government trusted that by acting in the manner suggested in the *Aide Memoire*, civil servants would earn the gratitude, admiration and respect of the general public.

In the end, the *Aide Memoire* concluded with the request that all occasions be utilised by senior officers to impress the discussed matters upon those working under them. It was necessary to ensure that lapses were taken notice of. If one lapse was ignored, a chain of reactions followed disturbing the balance of orderliness. Services did need a toning-up. It was also essential to create a proper understanding about the services in the public mind. The government expressed the hope that with tact and the sympathetic handling of the staff by senior administrative officers and by ensuring proper standards among them day today administrative difficulties and criticisms would greatly be surmounted.

The following poem by Thomas T. Lynch is also relevant in this connection:

"Lord, I on every day
With grateful heart would say,
"Thy truth are sure and beautiful;
How can my life grow dull?"

And when I eat and drink,
I joyfully would think,
That all thou hast created good
May be a wise man's food.

And as I work and trade,
Pay others, and am paid,
"Knowledge," I'll say, "we must not cease
To exchange, and so increase."

And when I hear the crowd
In busy traffic loud,
I'll cry, "How sweet would be the sound
Were all but brothers found!"

And when my friends at night
Count my return delight,
I'll think how pleased my God will be
His child in Heaven to see.

BIBLIOGRAPHY

1. Public Personal Administration, by O. Glenn Static, Fifth Edition of the earlier work by Williams E. Mosher, J Donall Kingsley and O.Glon Stave, Harper & Row Publishers, New York. Oxford & IBH Publishing Company, 36 Chorangee Road, Calcutta-16.
2. Beware the Naked Man who Offers you his Shirt, Hawrey Mackey-William Morrow & Co., Distributors.
3. Study of Philosophy: Will Durant.
4. High Visibility: Irvin J. RHW Philip Kotlar and Martin Stoller, Published by William Heinemann Ltd.
5. Enquire Within Modern Etiquette, by Moyer C. Chancellor Breasner Bern.
6. The Story of Philosophy, by Will Doronj, page 427, J R Kadica Nietzsene.
7. Cecil O Code, Significant Research on Leadership.
8. Peter F. Druker, Mandarin, The New Realities, India Book House.

Periodicals/Newspapers

1. The Indian Express: Weekend: The Leader in You-Vijay Ghosh, July 2, 1990.
2. The Times of India, How to Optimise Leadership, Business Terms Staff, 12 Jan. 1994.
3. The Economic Times, Leadership: Competence and Beyond, 9 Aug. 1990.
4. The Economic Times, Harish Puri—Leadership most talked least understood, by KRK Moorthy, Padmanabhan, 7 Aug. 1990, 13 Sept. 1990.
5. The Hindustan Times, Mrinalini Sarabhai, 24 Sept. 1989.
6. The Hindu, August 2, 1990.

7. The Illustrated Weekly of India, OW Excellence, October 1, 1978.

Reference/News Magazines/Periodicals/Newspapers

1. The Economic Times, Leadership Competence and Beyond-Harish Puri, 9 Aug. 1990.
2. The Economic Times, Leadership-Most Talked, Least Understood, by K.R.K. Moorthy, 9 Aug, 1990
3. The Economic Times: Nov. 8, 1990

The Indian Express Weekend, "The Leader in you", by Vijaya Ghosh, July 2, 1990.

The Economic Times, Leadership: Competence and beyond, Harish Puri, 9 July 1996.

The Indian Express, Week End, July 2, 1990, The Leader in You, Vijaya Ghosh.

The Hindustan Times, Saturday Magazine, September 23, 1989.

Mrinalini Sarabhai

The Economic Times: November 8, 1990.

INDEX